Rodgers & Hammerstein's

THE KING AND I

The Applause Libretto Library

Rodgers & Hammerstein's

THE KING
AND I

*The Complete Book and Lyrics
of the Broadway Musical*

Music by Richard Rodgers
Book and Lyrics by Oscar Hammerstein II
Based on the novel *Anna and the King of Siam*
by Margaret Landon

AN IMPRINT OF HAL LEONARD LLC

Published in 2016 by Applause Theatre & Cinema Books
An Imprint of Hal Leonard LLC
7777 West Bluemound Road
Milwaukee, WI 53213

Trade Book Division Editorial Offices
33 Plymouth St., Montclair, NJ 07042

Printed in the United States of America

Book compositor: UB Communications

Library of Congress Cataloging-in-Publication Data

Names: Hammerstein, Oscar, II, 1895-1960, author. | Libretto for (work):
   Rodgers, Richard, 1902-1979. King and I. | Libretto based on (work):
   Landon, Margaret, 1903-1993. Anna and the King of Siam.
Title: The king & I : the complete book and lyrics of the Broadway musical /
   music by Richard Rodgers ; book and lyrics by Oscar Hammerstein II ; based
   on Anna and the King of Siam by Margaret Landon.
Other titles: King and I | King and I
Description: Montclair : Applause Theatre & Cinema Books, 2016.
Identifiers: LCCN 2016019113 | ISBN 9781495056093 (pbk. : alk. paper)
Subjects: LCSH: Musicals—Librettos. | Leonowens, Anna Harriette,
   1831-1915—Drama. | Mongkut, King of Siam, 1804-1868—Drama.
Classification: LCC ML50.R67 K5 2016 | DDC 782.1/40268—dc23
LC record available at https://lccn.loc.gov/2016019113

ISBN 978-1-4950-5609-3

www.applausebooks.com

To Trude Rittman and Robert Russell Bennett
Key members of the musical team

CONTENTS

INTRODUCTION

There were a few weeks during the writing of *Cinderella* when Oscar Hammerstein II and Richard Rodgers were on opposite sides of the world. Rodgers was in New York, and Hammerstein had traveled with his Tasmanian wife, Dorothy, to the Summer Olympics in Melbourne, Australia. The pressure was on—CBS had announced *Cinderella* in September 1956 for a live broadcast the following March, and nothing had been written. So letters were exchanged, going into some detail, mostly about the song "Do I Love You Because You're Beautiful?" They are extraordinary and provide a glimpse into how the partnership worked, how the two men asked the other's opinions of thoughts and ideas, and how they questioned aspects of each other's contributions. But there was also shop talk and some personal comments. In one letter, dated November 28, Hammerstein begins with the following: "Last night I saw the picture 'The King And I' again. This morning I am convinced that this is our best work. I have a kind of humble feeling of not knowing how we did it. It has more wisdom as well as heart than any other musical play by anybody. It will remain 'modern' long after any of our other plays."

Of course that was before *Cinderella* was completed, and before either *Flower Drum Song* or *The Sound of Music*. But I am not sure he would have changed his opinion had he written those words later on.

The King and I was the follow-up to the enormous success of *South Pacific*. True to form, and to their genius, Rodgers and Hammerstein didn't try and write another *South Pacific*. *The King and I* is very different—and marked an interesting artistic step forward. While *South Pacific* had some old razzle-dazzle among its heartfelt story and dangerous setting, *The King and I* is more stately. After all, it is set in a very formal place, where "Honey Bun" would not have been welcomed. The court of Siam called for a formality—and one of R&H's inspired moves was to hire Jerome Robbins to handle the dances. In addition to some brilliantly modest staging for "Getting to Know You" and for the court itself, he created quite a masterpiece. "The Small House of Uncle Thomas" is a full ballet, conceived as an entertainment created by the slave Tuptim, the new gift to the King from the King of Burma, to present before the visiting English. She has become aware of Harriet Beecher Stowe's book about slavery ("A woman has written a book?" asks the King . . .) and wants Mrs. Anna to give her a copy. Tuptim uses the book as the basis for "her" show, which puts the King in an awkward light since it is about a slave escaping from a "wicked King"— something she is intending to do with her lover, Lun Tha. Rodgers' trusted dance arranger, Trude Rittmann, worked closely with Robbins, whose dance is in a style all of its own, liberally influenced by various Eastern dance traditions but with an underbelly of both theatricality and brazen storytelling. It is a masterpiece of musical theater choreography that has never been equaled.

There is indeed wisdom in *The King and I*. This is a story, based on fact, of the leader of an Eastern country who invites as a tutor to his many children a member of the Western world. King Mongkut actually did that, and it was the memoirs of the tutor herself (*An English Governess in the Court Of Siam*) that began the journey through a novelization and film (*Anna and the King of Siam*) to the hands of Rodgers and Hammerstein. Mongkut was bombastic, yet curious and questioning—and Mrs. Anna was brazen, yet determined and smart. Their relationship in the musical is extraordinary. Here is an exchange that reflects both their relationship and the wisdom of the show: When Mrs. Anna finds the King reading the Bible, he questions what it says, that the whole world was created in six days, when everyone knows it took many ages. She answers, "The Bible was not written by men of science, but by men of faith. It was their explanation of the miracle of creation, which is the same miracle—whether it took six days or many centuries." He is a King who knows exactly what he wants—or so he thinks, until something makes him think things through in a different light. His son, the crown prince, asks him how can it be that many people know one thing and yet something else is true. "Some day you, too, will be King, you too will know everything," he says, not really convincing himself. She is a woman with strong ideas and few fears. If theirs is a love story—as we come close to believing in "Shall We Dance?"—it is close to a non-love love story. Despite their affection for each other, she pushes too hard, and he hasn't the personal resources to adjust tradition to the modern world. But still, the real emotion at the end is the result of a rich story very well told.

Because of the phenomenon of *South Pacific*, many critics made the unfortunate mistake of making the comparison. "It must be reported," began Brooks Atkinson's review in the *New York Times*, "that *The King and I* is no match for *South Pacific*." Richard Watts Jr. of the *New York Post* put it right out there: "Unfairly but inevitably, everyone will want to know if it as good as *South Pacific*, and I will confess that I don't suppose it is." But reviews also said this: "*The King and I* is a beautiful and lovable musical play." "*The King and I* is a lovely and exciting achievement, of unusual taste and imagination, and a great credit to its distinguished authors and the American theatre." Those two quotes are from, well, Brooks Atkinson and Richard Watts Jr. Too bad they didn't have the confidence to state their praise of the show at the beginning of their reviews. These are the kinds of things that give Broadway producers ulcers.

Ted Chapin
The Rodgers & Hammerstein Organization

THE KING AND I

The Applause Libretto Library Series

THE KING AND I *was first produced by Richard Rodgers and Oscar Hammerstein II, on March 29, 1951, at the St. James Theatre, New York City, with the following cast:*

CAPTAIN ORTON .... Charles Francis

LOUIS LEONOWENS .... Sandy Kennedy

ANNA LEONOWENS .... Gertrude Lawrence

THE INTERPRETER .... Leonard Graves

THE KRALAHOME .... John Juliano

THE KING .... Yul Brynner

PHRA ALACK .... Len Mence

TUPTIM .... Doretta Morrow

LADY THIANG .... Dorothy Sarnoff

PRINCE CHULALONGKORN .... Johnny Stewart

PRINCESS YING YAOWALAK .... Baayork Lee

LUN THA .... Larry Douglas

SIR EDWARD RAMSAY .... Robin Craven

PRINCESSES AND PRINCES: Crisanta Cornejo, Andrea Del Rosario, Marjorie James, Barbara Luna, Nora Baez, Corrine St. Denis, Bunny Warner, Rodolfo Cornejo, Robert Cortazal, Thomas Griffin, Alfonso Maribo, James Maribo, Orlando Rodriguez

THE ROYAL DANCERS: Jamie Bauer, Lee Becker, Mary Burr, Gemze DeLappe, Shellie Farrell, Marilyn Gennaro, Evelyn Giles, Ina Kurland, Nancy Lynch, Michiko, Helen Murielle, Prue Ward, Dusty Worrall and Yuriko

WIVES: Stephanie Augustine, Marcia James, Ruth Korda, Suzanne Lake, Gloria Marlowe, Carolyn Maye, Helen Merritt, Phyllis Wilcox

AMAZONS: Geraldine Hamburg, Maribel Hammer, Norma Larkin, Miriam Lawrence

PRIESTS: Duane Camp, Joseph Caruso, Leonard Graves, Jack Matthew, Ed Preston

SLAVES: Doria Avila, Ravl Celeda, Beau Cunningham, Tommy Gomez

Directed by John van Druten
Choreography by Jerome Robbins
Settings and Lighting by Jo Mielziner
Costumes designed by Irene Sharaff
Orchestrations by Robert Russell Bennett
Ballet arrangements by Trude Rittmann
Musical Director, Frederick Dvonch

The play is divided into two acts. The action takes place in and around the King's palace, Bangkok, Siam.
Time: Early eighteen sixties.

ACT 1

SCENE 1

Deck of the Chow Phya, *a ship that has sailed from Singapore, up the Gulf of Siam, and is now making its way slowly along the winding river that approaches Bangkok.*

CAPTAIN ORTON, *a middle-aged Englishman, is leaning on the binnacle, smoking a pipe. The deck is crowded with boxes and crates of furniture.*

As soon as the curtain is up LOUIS *runs on.*

ORTON

Hello, laddy.

LOUIS
(*Mounting the steps of the gangway, to look out on the river*)
How near are we to Bangkok, Captain?

ORTON

See that cluster of lights jutting out into the river? That's it. That's Bangkok.

LOUIS
(*Seeing the crates and boxes*)
Oh, look! All our boxes!

ORTON

Aye, and a fair lot they are.

LOUIS

We packed everything we had in our Singapore house—furniture and everything.

ANNA
(*Offstage*)

Louis! Where are you?

LOUIS
(*Running to meet her as she enters*)

Mother! Mother, look! There's Bangkok! Do you see, Mother? That cluster of lights that sticks out into the river. You see, Mother? That's Bangkok!

ANNA
(*Laughing*)

I see, Louis. I see them. It's exciting, isn't it?

LOUIS

Will the King of Siam come down to the dock to meet us?

ANNA

The King himself? I don't think so. Kings don't as a rule.

ORTON
(*With earnest concern*)

I wonder if you know what you're facing, Ma'am—an English-woman here in the East . . .

LOUIS
(*Running down right, looking out toward the audience, and pointing over the imaginary rail*)

Look, Mother! Look at that boat! Look at the dragon's head in the bow, and all the men standing up, carrying torches.

ORTON

That's the Royal Barge!

LOUIS

Do you suppose that's the King, the man sitting under the gold canopy?

ORTON

That's the Kralahome. (*Explaining to* ANNA) Sort of "Prime Minster"—the King's right-hand man, you might say.

ANNA

Do you suppose he's coming out to meet us?

ORTON

No doubt of it. They'll be waiting till we pass them. Then they'll come around our stern. (*He starts to go, then turns back*) Ma'am . . . if I might be allowed to offer you a word of warning . . .

ANNA

What is it, Captain?

ORTON
(*Indicating the barge*)
That man has power, and he can use it *for* you or *against* you.

ANNA
(*Laughing*)

Oh.

ORTON

I think you should know.
> (*He goes off. A sound comes from the river, a snarling sound in rhythm, oarsmen marking the cadence of their stroke.*)

LOUIS

Look, Mother! They're closer! (*With amazement, as he gets a better view*) Mother! The Prime Minister is naked!

ANNA

Hush, Louis, that's not a nice word. He's not naked. (*She looks again*) Well, he's *half* naked.

LOUIS

They all look rather horrible, don't they, Mother? (*He draws a little closer to her*) Father would not have liked us to be afraid, would he?

ANNA

No, Louis. Father would not have liked us to be afraid.

LOUIS

Mother, does anything ever frighten you?

ANNA

Sometimes.

LOUIS

What do you do?

ANNA

I whistle.

LOUIS

Oh, that's why you whistle!

ANNA

(*Laughing*)

Yes, that's why I whistle . . .
  (*She sings:*)
  Whenever I feel afraid
  I hold my head erect
  And whistle a happy tune,
  So no one will suspect
  I'm afraid.

  While shivering in my shoes
  I strike a careless pose
  And whistle a happy tune,
  And no one ever knows
  I'm afraid.

  The result of this deception
  Is very strange to tell,
  For when I fool the people I fear
  I fool myself as well!

  I whistle a happy tune,
  And ev'ry single time
  The happiness in the tune
  Convinces me that I'm
  Not afraid!

  Make believe you're brave
  And the trick will take you far;

You may be as brave
As you make believe you are.
    (LOUIS *whistles this strain, then they both sing:*)

ANNA AND LOUIS

You may be as brave
As you make believe you are.

LOUIS

(*After a moment's reflection*)
I think that's a very good idea, Mother. A very good idea.

ANNA

It *is* a good idea, isn't it?

LOUIS

I don't think I shall ever be afraid again.

ANNA

Good!
    (LOUIS *resumes singing the refrain.* ANNA *joins in. They do not
    see four Siamese slaves, naked from the waist up, with knives
    in their belts, come over the rail, down the gangway, and line
    up, center. As they are happily singing the last eight measures*
    ANNA *turns, sees the formidable-looking Siamese, and gasps
    in terror.* LOUIS *sees them, too, and clutches his mother's arm.
    Then they face the men and whistle—as casually as they can.*)

ORTON

(*Coming on hurriedly, followed by two deckhands*)
Clear that away! (*The deckhands remove a trunk*) Ma'am, I wouldn't
whistle. He might think it disrespectful.

ANNA

Oh, was I whistling? Sorry, I didn't realize.
(*The* INTERPRETER *comes over the rail and down the steps.*)

INTERPRETER
(*Rather insolently, to* ANNA)
Good evening, sir. Welcome to Siam.
(*He turns his back on her and prostrates himself, toad-like, as do the four slaves.*)

LOUIS

He called you sir!

ANNA

Hush, dear! Hush!
(*The* KRALAHOME *comes over the rail slowly and with terrifying majesty. He is naked from the waist up, except for several necklaces. Now he addresses the* INTERPRETER *in Siamese.*)

(*At this point, and throughout the play, the Siamese language will be represented by certain sounds made in the orchestra. Siamese words will never be literally pronounced. music will symbolize them.*)

INTERPRETER
(*Turning to* ANNA, *still crouching like a toad, relaying the* KRALAHOME'*s questions*)
Sir, His Excellency wishes to know—are you lady who will be schoolmistress of royal children?

ANNA
(*In a small, frightened voice*)
Yes.

INTERPRETER

Have you friends in Bangkok?

ANNA

I know no one in Bangkok at all.
(*The* INTERPRETER *delivers her answers and the* KRALAHOME
directs him to ask further questions.)

INTERPRETER

Are you married, sir?

ANNA

I am a widow.

INTERPRETER

What manner of man your deceased husband?

ANNA

My husband was an officer of Her Majesty's Army in . . . (*She
suddenly stiffens*) Tell your master his business with me is in my
capacity of schoolteacher to the royal children. He has no right
to pry into my personal affairs. (ORTON *tries to signal a warning,
but she turns to him impatiently*) Well, he hasn't, Captain Orton!
(*The* INTERPRETER *gives the* KRALAHOME *her message. The*
KRALAHOME *gives the* INTERPRETER *a kick on the shoulder
which sends him sprawling out of the way.*)

LOUIS

(*To* ANNA, *pointing toward the* KRALAHOME)
I don't like that man!

KRALAHOME

In foreign country is best you like everyone—until you leave.

ANNA
(*Startled*)
Your Excellency, I had no idea you spoke English.

KRALAHOME
It is not necessary for you to know everything at once. You come
with me now. Your boxes are carried to palace—later.

ANNA
No. Not to the palace. I am not living at the palace.

KRALAHOME
Who say?

ANNA
The King say . . . Says! The King has promised me twenty pounds
a month and a house of my own.

KRALAHOME
King do not always remember what he promise. If I tell him he
break his promise, I will make anger in him. I think it is better I
make anger in him about larger matters.

ANNA
But all I want is ten minutes' audience with him.

KRALAHOME
King very busy now. New Year's celebrations just finishing. Fireworks every night. Cremation of late Queen just starting.

ANNA
Oh. You have lost your Queen. I am so sorry. When did she die?

KRALAHOME

Four years ago . . . With cremation ceremony comes also fire-works.

ANNA

And what am I to do in the meantime?

KRALAHOME

In the meantime you wait—in palace.

ANNA

(*Firmly*)

Your Excellency, I will *teach* in the palace, but I must have a house of my own—where I can go at the end of the day when my duties are over.

KRALAHOME

What you wish to do in evening that cannot be done in palace?

ANNA

How dare you! (*Controlling herself*) I'm sorry, Your Excellency, but you don't understand. I came here to work. I must support myself and my young son. And I shall take nothing less than what I have been promised.

KRALAHOME

You will tell King this?

ANNA

I will tell King this.
(*The faint suggestion of a smile curls the corner of the* KRALAHOME'*s mouth.*)

KRALAHOME

It will be very interesting meeting . . . You come now? (ANNA *does not answer*) You come now, or you can stay on boat. I do not care! (*He turns toward gangway and starts to go.*)

ORTON
(*Going to* ANNA *sympathetically*)
If you wish to stay on my ship and return to Singapore, Ma'am . . .

ANNA

No, thank you, Captain Orton. (*Calling to the* KRALAHOME) Your Excellency—(*The* KRALAHOME *stops and turns*) I will go with you. I have made a bargain, and I shall live up to my part of it. But I expect a bargain to be kept on both sides. I shall go with you, Your Excellency.

KRALAHOME

To the palace?

ANNA
(*Grimly, after a pause*)
For the time being. (*The* KRALAHOME *smiles and exits over the ship's rail.* ANNA *turns to* ORTON) Good-bye, Captain Orton, and thank you very much for everything. (*Turning to* LOUIS, *prompting him*) Louis!

LOUIS
(*Shaking hands*)
Good-bye, Captain.

ORTON

Good-bye, laddy.

(*As they turn from the captain,* ANNA *and* LOUIS *are confronted by the* INTERPRETER *and the slaves standing in a stern line, their arms folded, their faces glowering in a most unfriendly manner.* ANNA *and* LOUIS *pause, then raise their chins and whistle "a happy tune" as they walk by the men and start to climb the gangway.*)

INTERMEDIATE SCENE

A Palace corridor.

Several court dancers have their costumes adjusted and last-minute touches added to their faces by make-up experts. Excitement, haste and anxiety pervade the scene. An attendant enters and claps his hands. The dancers bustle off promptly, their attendants making their exit on the opposite side.

SCENE 2

The KING's study in the royal palace.

    As the curtain rises the KING is seated cross-legged on a low table, dictating letters to PHRA ALACK, his secretary, and paying only scant attention to a group of girl dancers. At length he throws the last letter at the secretary, rises and snaps his fingers. The secretary and the dancers retire quickly. The KING beckons to someone offstage. The KRALAHOME enters.

KRALAHOME

Your Majesty . . .

KING

Well, well, well?

KRALAHOME

I have been meaning to speak to you about English schoolteacher. She is waiting to see you.

KING

She is in Siam? How long?

KRALAHOME

Two weeks, three weeks. She has needed disciplining, Your Majesty. She objects to living in palace. Talks about house she say you promise her.

KING

I do not recollect such promise. Tell her I will see her. I will see her in a moment. (*Over the KRALAHOME's shoulder, the KING sees LUN THA enter, preceded by a female palace attendant*) Who? Who? Who?

KRALAHOME

Your Majesty, this is Lun Tha, emissary from court of Burma.

KING

Ah! You are here for copying of famous Bangkok temple. (*To* KRALAHOME) I have give permission.

KRALAHOME

(*As* TUPTIM *is carried on, on a palanquin,
by four Amazons*)

He brings you present from Prince of Burma.

KING

Am I to trust a ruler of Burma? Am I to trust this present they send me, or is she a spy?

TUPTIM

(*Rising from palanquin*)

I am not a spy . . . My name is Tuptim. You are pleased that I speak English? My name is Tuptim.

(*The* KING *looks at her appraisingly. The* KRALAHOME *signals for her to turn around. She does so. The* KING *walks around her slowly, darts a brief, enigmatic look at the* KRALAHOME, *and walks off.*)

KRALAHOME

King is pleased with you. He likes you.

(*He dismisses* LUN THA *and leaves. Before going out,* LUN THA *exchanges a worried, helpless look with* TUPTIM. TUPTIM *turns and looks toward where the* KING *made his exit, bitterness and hatred in her eyes.*)

TUPTIM

The King is pleased!
   (*She sings:*)
He is pleased with me!
My lord and master
Declares he's pleased with me—
What does he mean?
What does he know of me,
This lord and master?
When he has looked at me
What has he seen?
   Something young,
   Soft and slim,
   Painted cheek,
   Tap'ring limb,
   Smiling lips
   All for him,
   Eyes that shine
   Just for him—
So he thinks . . .
Just for him!
Though the man may be
My Lord and Master,
Though he may study me
As hard as he can,
The smile beneath my smile
He'll never see.
He'll never know I love
Another man,
He'll never know
I love another man!

(*The* KING *enters.* TUPTIM *immediately resumes her humble and obedient attitude*)
Your Majesty wishes me to leave?

KING

I will tell you when I wish you to leave.

KRALAHOME
(*Entering, ushering in* ANNA, *who is followed by two Amazons*)
Schoolteacher.
(ANNA *comes before the* KING *and curtseys*)
Madame Leonowens.

KING

You are schoolteacher?

ANNA

Yes, Your Majesty, I am schoolteacher. When can I start my work?

KING

You can start when I tell you to start.

ANNA

There is one matter we have to settle, Your Majesty . . .

KING
(*Interrupting her*)
You are part of general plan I have for bringing to Siam what is good in Western culture. Already I have bring printing press here—for printing.

ANNA

Yes, I know, Your Majesty.

KING

How you know?

ANNA

Before I signed our agreement, I found out all I could about Your Majesty's ambitions for Siam.

KING

Ha! This is scientific. (*He squints at her thoughtfully*) You are pleased with your apartments in palace?

ANNA

They . . . are quite comfortable, Your Majesty. (*Exchanging a look with the* KRALAHOME) For the time being. But my young son and I have found it rather . . . confining . . . with Amazons guarding the doors and not permitting us to leave.

KING

Strangers cannot be allowed to roam around palace before presentment to King. You could look out of windows.

ANNA

Yes, Your Majesty, we have done that. We have seen New Year celebrations, royal cremation ceremonies, etcetera, etcetera.

KING

What is this "etcetera"?

ANNA

According to the dictionary, it means "and the rest," Your Majesty. All the things you have been doing while we were waiting. The fireworks—

KING

Best fireworks I ever see at funeral. How you like my acrobats?

ANNA

Splendid, Your Majesty. Best acrobats I have ever seen at funeral.

KING

(*Pleased*)

Ha! (*To* KRALAHOME) Have children prepare for presentation to schoolteacher.

ANNA

How many children have you, Your Majesty?

KING

I have only sixty-seven altogether. I begin very late. But you shall not teach all of them. You shall teach only children of mothers who are in favor of King . . .

(LADY THIANG *has entered. She prostrates herself before the* KING)

Ah! Lady Thiang. Madame Leonowens, this is Lady Thiang, head wife.

(*She immediately and quite irrelevantly starts to sing.*)

THIANG

There is a happy land, far, far away,
Where saints in glory stand, bright, bright as day.
(*Speaking*)
In the beginning God created the heaven and the earth.
(ANNA *looks puzzled*)
Mis-son-ary.

ANNA

A missionary taught you English!

THIANG

Yes, sir. Mis-son-ary.

KING

Lady Thiang, you will help Madame Leonowens with her schoolteaching, and she in her turn shall teach you the better English.
>   (THIANG *prostrates herself at the feet of the* KING, *to* ANNA's *surprise and horror. The* KING *explains:*)
She is grateful to me for my kindness.

ANNA

I see. (*Getting back to the issue she is so anxious to settle*) Your Majesty, in our agreement, you . . .

KING

(*Talking across* ANNA)

You, Tuptim. You already speak well the English. (TUPTIM *rises. The* KING *turns to* ANNA, *pointing to* TUPTIM) She arrive today. She is present to me from Burma prince.

ANNA

(*Shocked*)

She is a present?

TUPTIM

Madame, you have English books I can read?

ANNA

Of course I have.

TUPTIM

I wish most to read book called "The Small House of Uncle Thomas." Is by American lady, Harriet Beecher Stowa.

KING

A woman has written a book?

ANNA

A very wonderful book, Your Majesty. All about slavery . . .

KING

Ha! President Lingkong against slavery, no? Me, too. Slavery very bad thing.
> (ANNA *looks significantly at the prostrate figure of* LADY THIANG. *The* KING *snaps his fingers and* LADY THIANG *rises. The* KING *paces thoughtfully, speaking half to himself, half to* ANNA)
I think you will teach my wives too—those wives who are in favor.
> (*During the ensuing dialogue, small groups of the* KING's *wives peek in through the entrances and retreat, as if curious to hear and see, but afraid of the* KING's *mounting temper.*)

ANNA

I shall be most happy to teach your wives, even though that was not part of our agreement. . . . Speaking of our agreement reminds me that there is one little matter, about my house . . .

KING

Also, I will allow you to help me in my foreign correspondence.

ANNA

Yes, Your Majesty. I don't think you understand about the house, Your Majesty. For the time being . . .

KING
(*Wheeling around suddenly*)
House? House? What is this about house?

ANNA
(*Startled, then recovering*)
I want my house! The house you promised me, Your Majesty.

KING
You shall live in palace. You teach in palace, you shall live in palace. If you do not live in palace, you do not teach, and you go—wherever you please. I do not care. You understand this?

ANNA
I understand, but, Your Majesty, if these are the only terms on which I . . .

KING
Enough! I have no more time to talk. Talk to other women, my women—my wives.
(*He snaps his fingers at* TUPTIM, *who follows him obediently as he exits. As soon as the* KING *has left, the wives rush on from all sides, chattering excitedly. They surround* ANNA, *taking her gloves and her reticule, fingering her clothes. Two on the floor try to lift up her skirt.*)

ANNA
For goodness' sake! What is the matter? What are they trying to do to me?

THIANG
They think you wear big skirt like that because you shaped like that.

ANNA

Well, I'm not!

(*She lifts her hoop skirt, revealing pantalettes. Two wives address* LADY THIANG, *the orchestra, as usual, playing sounds to indicate the Siamese language.*)

THIANG

They wish to know, sir, if you have children?

ANNA

(*Indicating his size*)

One little boy.

THIANG

(*Proudly*)

I have boy, too—Crown Prince Chowfa Chulalongkorn, heir to throne . . . (*An earnest pleading coming into her voice*) I would be happy if you would teach children.

ANNA

I would like to very much. I came all the way here from Singapore to do so, but I really cannot . . .

THIANG

You could be great help to all here, sir.

ANNA

Lady Thiang, why do you call me "sir"?

THIANG

Because you scientific. Not lowly, like woman.

ANNA

Do you *all* think women are more lowly than men?
(THIANG *translates this to the wives, all of whom smile broadly and nod their heads, apparently quite happy with the idea of female inferiority.* ANNA*'s voice is indignant*)
Well, I don't.

THIANG

Please, sir, do not tell King. Make King angry.

ANNA

King seems to be angry already. (*Thoughtfully*) That lovely girl.
He said she was a present . . .

THIANG

From court of Burma. I think she love another man. If so, she
will never see other man again.

ANNA

Poor child!

THIANG

Oh, no, sir! She is foolish child, to wish for another man when
she has King.

ANNA

But you can't help wishing for a man, if he's the man you want.

THIANG

It is strange for schoolteacher to talk so—romantic.

ANNA

(*Smiling*)

Romantic! I suppose I am. I was very much in love with my husband, Tom.

THIANG

Tom.

(*She translates this to the wives, who repeat after her, "Tom."*)

ANNA

Once a woman has loved like that, she understands all other women who are in love . . . and she's on their side, even if she's . . . a schoolteacher.

(*The wives again pronounce "Tom" as if fascinated by the sound*)

Yes . . . Tom.

(*She opens the locket around her neck and shows it to* LADY THIANG.)

THIANG
(*Looking at the picture*)

He was pretty in face.

ANNA

Oh, dear, yes. He was very pretty in face.

(*She sings:*)
When I think of Tom
I think about a night
When the earth smelled of summer
And the sky was streaked with white,
And the soft mist of England
Was sleeping on a hill—
I remember this,
And I always will . . .

There are new lovers now on the same silent hill,
Looking on the same blue sea,
And I know Tom and I are a part of them all,
And they're all a part of Tom and me.
(*She is far away from them now, in another time, another place*)

Hello, young lovers, whoever you are,
I hope your troubles are few.
All my good wishes go with you tonight—
I've been in love like you.
Be brave, young lovers, and follow your star,
Be brave and faithful and true,
Cling very close to each other tonight—
I've been in love like you.
I know how it feels to have wings on your heels,
And to fly down a street in a trance.
You fly down a street on the chance that you'll meet,
And you meet—not really by chance.
Don't cry, young lovers, whatever you do,
Don't cry because I'm alone;
All of my memories are happy tonight,
I've had a love of my own,
I've had a love of my own, like yours—
I've had a love of my own.
(*Now there is a loud crash on a gong. The* KING *enters.*)

KING

The children! The children! (*To* ANNA) They come for presentment to schoolteacher.

ANNA

But, Your Majesty, we have not solved my problem . . .

KING

Silence! You will stand here to meet royal children. (*He indicates a place for her.*)

ANNA

(*Reluctantly accepting his order*)
Very well, Your Majesty.

KING

The Royal Princes and Princesses!

(*Now, to the strains of a patrol, the royal Siamese children enter, one by one, each advancing first to the* KING *and prostrating himself before his/her father, then rising, moving over to* ANNA, *and greeting her in the traditional manner by taking her two hands and pressing them to his/her forehead, after which he/ she backs away across the stage, and takes his/her place with the wives and children who have previously entered. Each succeeding child enters at about the time that his/her predecessor has greeted* ANNA *and is backing across the stage. The twins enter together, and the* KING *holds up two fingers to* ANNA, *so that she is sure to observe that they are twins. There are other variations. One little girl goes straight to her father, her arms outstretched, but he sternly points to the floor. She prostrates herself in the formal manner and, very much abashed, goes on to* ANNA. *One little girl, who had been delegated to give* ANNA *a rose, forgets it the first time and has to run back to* ANNA, *disgraced by her absentmindedness. The most impressive moment is the entrance of the Crown Prince,* CHULALONGKORN. *The music becomes loud and brave at this point. Then, toward the end of the patrol, the music becomes softer and ends with the smallest children coming on, the last child backing up and bowing with the others on the last beat of the music. Throughout this procession,* ANNA *has obviously fallen more and more in love with the children. She is deeply touched by their courtesy, their charm, their sweetness. After they have all bowed to her and the* KING, *she slowly moves to the center of the room. She looks back at the* KING, *who nods understandingly, and then slowly she starts to untie the ribbons of her bonnet. As she takes out the pin and lifts the bonnet off her head, one little child gasps an excited "ah," and the children with one accord all rush up to her and surround her. She leans over and hugs all those she can reach, and it is obvious that they are going to be fast friends as the curtain closes.)*

SCENE 3

In the Palace grounds.

A group of PRIESTS *chant as they walk by. From the other side the children enter singing "Home Sweet Home" as a counter-melody to the chant. They walk two by two, in time to the music. The* PRIESTS *exit. The* KING *enters and gestures to* CHULALONGKORN *to step out of line. The* PRINCE *obeys. The other children continue off-stage.*

CHULALONGKORN

Father, I shall be late for school.

KING

You wait! (*There is angry purpose in his voice and manner*) Please to recite proverb you have learned yesterday and writing down twelve times in your copybook.

CHULALONGKORN

"A thought for the day: East or West, home is best."

KING

East, West, home best. Means house! Every day for many, many months! Always something about house! Are my children to be taught nothing more?

CHULALONGKORN

Yesterday we are taught that the world is a round ball which spins on a stick through the middle. (*He looks at the* KING *to see the effect of this outrageous statement*) Everyone knows that the world rides on the back of a great turtle, who keeps it from running into the stars.

KING

How can it be that everyone knows one thing, if many people believe another thing?

CHULALONGKORN

Then which is true? (*Pause*)

KING

The world is a ball with stick through it . . . I believe.

CHULALONGKORN

You believe? Does that mean you do not *know*? (*His father does not answer*) But you must know, because you are King.

KING

Good. Some day you, too, will be King and you too will know everything.

CHULALONGKORN

But how do I learn? And when do I know that I know everything?

KING

When you are King. Now leave me.
    (CHULALONGKORN *goes out. The* KING *soliloquizes*)
When you are King. But *I* do not know. I am not sure. I am not sure of anything.
    (*He sings:*)
    When I was a boy
    World was better spot.
    What was so was so,
    What was not was not.
    Now I am a man—

World have change a lot:
Some things *nearly* so,
Others *nearly* not.

There are times I almost think
I am not sure of what I absolutely know.
Very often find confusion
In conclusion I concluded long ago.
In my head are many facts
That, as a student, I have studied to procure.
In my head are many facts
Of which I wish I was more certain I was sure!
    (*He speaks:*)
Is a puzzlement! What to tell a growing son!
    (*He sings:*)
What, for instance, shall I say to him of women?
Shall I educate him on the ancient lines?
Shall I tell the boy, as far as he is able,
To respect his wives and love his concubines?
Shall I tell him every one is like the other,
And the better one of two is really neither?
If I tell him this I think he won't believe it—
And I nearly think I don't believe it either!

When my father was a king
He was a king who knew exactly what he knew,
And his brain was not a thing
Forever swinging to and fro and fro and to.
Shall I, then, be like my father
And be willfully unmovable and strong?
Or is better to be right?
Or am I right when I believe I may be wrong?

Shall I join with other nations in alliance?
If allies are weak, am I not best alone?
If allies are strong with power to protect me,
Might they not protect me out of all I own?
Is a danger to be trusting one another,
One will seldom want to do what other wishes . . .
But unless some day somebody trust somebody,
There'll be nothing left on earth excepting fishes!

There are times I almost think
Nobody sure of what he absolutely know.
Everybody find confusion
In conclusion he concluded long ago,
And it puzzle me to learn
That though a man may be in doubt of what he know,
Very quickly will he fight,
He'll fight to prove that what he does not know is so!

Oh-h-h-h-h-h!
Sometimes I think that people going mad!
Ah-h-h-h-h-h!
Sometimes I think that people not so bad!
But no matter what I think
I must go on living life.
As leader of my kingdom I must go forth,
Be father to my children,
And husband to each wife—
Etcetera, etcetera, and so forth.
     (*His arms and eyes raised in prayer*)
If my Lord in Heaven, Buddha, show the way,
Every day I try to live another day.
If my Lord in Heaven, Buddha, show the way,

Every day I do my best—for one more day!
  (*His arms and shoulders droop. He speaks the last line:*)
But . . . is a puzzlement!
  (*The lights go out. The voices of the* CHILDREN *are heard in the darkness, coming from the schoolroom.*)

SCENE 4

The Schoolroom. Up center is a large stand with a map hanging from it. This is an ancient map, showing a very large Siam with a heroic figure of an armored king superimposed. Adjoining is a much smaller Burma, with a pathetic naked figure representing the king of that country.

The children are lined up singing their school song. LADY THIANG *and* TUPTIM *stand a little apart from the group, as does* LOUIS. CHULALONGKORN *is in the group with the children and wives.* ANNA *conducts them with a blackboard pointer. Soon after the curtain rises, she stops them in the middle of their song.*

ANNA

Spread out, children. (*They obey*) Now, that last line was "English words are all we speak." I didn't quite understand. I want to hear the beginnings and ends of your words. Once again, now, and nice big smiles because we love our school.

WIVES AND CHILDREN
(*Singing:*)

We work and work
From week to week
At the Royal Bangkok Academy.
And English words
Are all we speak
At the Royal Bangkok Academy.
If we pay
Attention to our teacher
And obey her every rule,
We'll be grateful for
These golden years
At our dear old school.

The Royal Bangkok Academy,
Our dear old school.

ANNA

That's fine. Now take your places.

(*The children sit, the bigger ones on the right, with* CHUL-
ALONGKORN *and* TUPTIM *behind them, the little ones down
center, their backs to the audience, facing* ANNA *who stands
up center. The wives line up on the left.*)

Lady Thiang, will you start?

(ANNA *hands the pointer to* LADY THIANG.)

THIANG

(*Using the pointer on the map*)

Blue is ocean. Red—Siam

(*Enthusiastic reaction from the children at Siam's great size*)

Here is King of Siam.

(*Indicating armored figure*)

In right hand is weapon—show how he destroy all who fight him.

(*More approval*)

Green—Burma.

(LADY THIANG *looks disapprovingly at* TUPTIM)

Here, King of Burma.

(*Indicating naked figure*)

No clothes mean how poor is King of Burma.

(*Children giggle.*)

ANNA

Thank you, Lady Thiang. Will you take my chair?

(LADY THIANG *sits.* ANNA *addresses the class:*)

The map you have been looking at is an old one. Today we have
a surprise. Louis—

(LOUIS *rolls down an 1862 world map in Mercator projection.*
The children gasp)
A new map—just arrived from England. It is a gift to us from
His Majesty, your King.

WIVES AND CHILDREN
(*Bowing in unison*)
The Lord of Light.

ANNA
Er—yes—The Lord of Light.

LOUIS
(*With the pointer*)
The white is Siam.
(*There is a groan of disbelief and disappointment from the
children and wives.*)

CHULALONGKORN
Siam not so small!

LOUIS
Wait! Let me show you England. (*Points*) See! It is even smaller
than Siam.
(*Children indicate approval.*)

ANNA
For many years, before I came here, Siam was to me that little
white spot. Now I have lived here for more than a year. I have
met the people of Siam. And I am learning to understand them.

A PRINCESS
You like us?

ANNA

I like you very much. Very much indeed.
　　(*The children express their delight.* ANNA *sings:*)
　It's a very ancient saying,
　But a true and honest thought,
　That "if you become a teacher
　By your pupils you'll be taught."
　As a teacher I've been learning
　(You'll forgive me if I boast)
　And I've now become an expert
　On the subject I like most:
　　(*She speaks:*)
Getting to know you . . .
　　(*She sings:*)
　Getting to know you,
　Getting to know all about you,
　Getting to like you,
　Getting to hope you like me,
　Getting to know you—
　Putting it my way, but nicely,
　You are precisely
　My cup of tea!
　Getting to know you,
　Getting to feel free and easy;
　When I am with you,
　Getting to know what to say—
　Haven't you noticed?
　Suddenly I'm bright and breezy
　Because of
　All the beautiful and new
　Things I'm learning about you,
　Day by day.

(*The refrain is taken up by the wives, Amazons and children.*
ANNA *teaches them handshaking, and* LADY THIANG *learns to
curtsey. One wife performs a dance with a fan and* ANNA,
*imitating her, dances with her. Then she dances with the
children. At the finish they are all seated on the floor, giggling.
She rises suddenly, remembering her duties*)

My goodness! This started out to be a lesson! Now, let's get back
to work!

(*They scurry back to their places.*)

CHULALONGKORN
(*Pointing to the map*)

What is that green up there?

ANNA

That is Norway. (*Repeating precisely for the benefit of her students*)
Nor-way.

WIVES AND CHILDREN
(*Imitating the sound*)

Nor-way.

ANNA

Norway is a very cold place. It is sometimes so cold that the
lakes and rivers freeze, and the water becomes so hard that you
can walk on it.

A SMALL PRINCE

Walk on water?

ANNA

Yes, walk on water.

CHULALONGKORN

How is it possible? Hard water!

ANNA

It is not only hard, but very slippery, too. When people walk on it, they fall down, and slide . . . (*General reaction of skepticism*) Not only do the lakes and rivers freeze, but the raindrops, as they fall, are changed into small white spots that look like lace! This is called snow.

TUPTIM
(*Fascinated*)

Snow?

WIVES AND CHILDREN
(*Another new word*)

Snow . . .

CHULALONGKORN
(*Not to be taken in*)

Spots of lace!

ANNA

Yes, Your Highness! The water freezes—on the way down from the sky.

CHULALONGKORN

And the raindrops turn into little stars!
    (*The pupils giggle, their credulity strained too far. The class becomes disorganized.*)

ANNA

Yes, Your Highness. Some are shaped like stars—small, white . . .
(*Bedlam is breaking loose.*)

PRINCESS YING YAOWALAK

I do not believe such thing as snow!
(*Cries of assent.*)

TWINS

(*Dividing the lines and gestures between them,
keeping two hands together*)
And I do not believe that Siam is this big—(*Indicating small size*)
And other country so big! (*Wide gesture.*)

CHULALONGKORN

Siam is biggest country in world!
(*Shouts, cartwheels, pandemonium greet this popular pronouncement.*)

KING

(*Entering suddenly*)
What? What? What?
(*All but* ANNA *and* LOUIS *instantly prostrate themselves. The* KING *stands for a moment in outraged silence*)
How can schoolroom be so . . . unscientific?

ANNA

Your Majesty, we have had a little misunderstanding. I was describing snow and they refused to believe that there was such a thing.

KING

Snow?

ANNA
(*Gathering snow falling*)

Snow.

(CHULALONGKORN *has raised his head and noted her gesture.*)

KING
(*Feeling his way*)

Oh, yes. From mountain top.

ANNA

From the sky.

KING

From sky *to* mountain top.

CHULALONGKORN

Sire . . . please . . . how does it come down from the sky?

KING

Like this. (*And he makes exactly the same gesture as* ANNA *did, lowering his hands and wiggling his fingers the while.*)

CHULALONGKORN
(*Gravely*)

Thank you, sire.

KING
(*He snaps his fingers as if bringing the picture
back to his mind*)

I have see picture—Switzerland!

ANNA

That's right, Your Majesty.

KING

Land all white—with snow. (*Turning to the class, with an angry challenge*) Who does not believe this? (*There is complete silence.*)

ANNA

Well, after all, they have never seen it, and . . .

KING

Never see? If they will know only what they see, why do we have schoolroom?
  (*He turns to the class and crackles out a sudden command*)
Rise!
  (*They all come to their feet*)
Do not ever let me hear of not believing teacher, who I have bring here at high expense—twenty pounds—each month.
  (*All eyes turn toward* ANNA *with a strange accusing look, as if she were robbing the* KING)
Twenty English pounds!
  (*He stamps his foot*)
Sterling!
  (*Not knowing what "sterling" means, but impressed by the sound as the* KING *shouts it, they all fall to the floor again*)
Children must learn.
  (*He turns to* ANNA)
Teacher must teach! Not waste time instructing children in silly English song "Home Sweet House"—to remind me of breaking promises that I never made, etcetera, etcetera, etcetera . . .

ANNA

  (*Summoning all her courage*)
Your Majesty . . . you did promise me a house.
  (*He glares at her, but she does not flinch*)

"A brick residence adjoining the royal palace." Those were your words in your letter.

KING

I do not remember such words.

ANNA

I remember them.

KING

I will do remembering. Who is King? I remind you—so you remember *that!* (*He is screaming now*) I do not know of any promises. I do not know anything but that you are my servant.

ANNA
(*Automatically resenting the word*)
Oh, no, Your Majesty!
(*There is a gasp of astonishment from those in the schoolroom.*)

KING

What? What? What? I say you are my servant!

ANNA

No, Your Majesty, that's not true. I most certainly am *not* your servant!

CHULALONGKORN
(*To* LOUIS)
I would say your mother has bad manners.

LOUIS

You would, would you? Well, I'd say your father has no manners at all!

ANNA

Louis! (*She takes his hand and turns to face the* KING) If you do not give me the house you promised, I shall return to England. (*There is a frightened murmur from her pupils.* ANNA, *herself, looks surprised at her own temerity.*)

PRINCESS SOMAWADI
(*Running to her*)

No! No! No!

PRINCE SUK SAWAT

Do not go to England!

PRINCE THONGKORN YAI
(*To the* KING)

We learn. We believe schoolteacher.

PRINCESS YING YAOWALAK

I believe in snow!

THIANG
(*To the* KING)

Do not let her go away.

KING

I let her do nothing, except what is my pleasure.
(*To* ANNA)
It is my pleasure you stay here. You stay here in palace. In palace!

ANNA

No, Your Majesty!

KING

(*Weakening a little*)

I give you servants. I give you bigger room.

ANNA

That is not the point, Your Majesty.

KING

Why do you wish to leave these children, all of whom are loving you so extraordinarily?

ANNA

I don't wish to leave them. I love them, too . . . quite extraordinarily. But I cannot stay in a country where a promise has no meaning.

KING

I will hear no more about this promise . . .

ANNA

A land where there is talk of honor, and a wish for Siam to take her place among the modern nations of the world! Where there is talk of great changes, but where everything still remains according to the wishes of the King!

KING

You will say no more!

ANNA

(*On the edge of tears*)

I will say no more, because—because I have no more to say. (*She starts off*) Come, Louis.

(*He follows her out, as the wives and children call after her:
"Please don't go, Mrs. Anna," etc. But she goes! The* KING
*stamps his foot angrily to silence them all. Then she shouts a
dismissal.*)

KING

Out! Out! Out!
(*They scurry out. The* KING's *thoughts are confused. He paces
up and down, then stops before the map. His voice is low and
thoughtful*)

So big a world! Siam very small . . . England very small . . . all
people very small. No man big enough for to be alone. No man
big enough! King? King different! King need no one . . . nobody
at all! (*Pause*) I think!
(*He leaves the room.*)
(*In a moment* TUPTIM *comes in. She looks around cautiously,
then sits on the floor with a book.* LUN THA *enters, then stops
quickly, surprised to find* TUPTIM *alone.*)

LUN THA

Where is Mrs. Anna?

TUPTIM

She will not be with us ever again. She has quarreled with the
King.

LUN THA

How can we meet if she is not with us? Mrs. Anna was our only
friend, and . . .

TUPTIM

We cannot be seen talking like this. Anyone can come in. Pretend
you wait for her.

LUN THA
(*Bitterly*)

If only we could stop pretending!
    (*He sings:*)
  We kiss in a shadow,
  We hide from the moon,
  Our meetings are few,
  And over too soon.
  We speak in a whisper,
  Afraid to be heard—
  When people are near
  We speak not a word!
  Alone in our secret,
  Together we sigh
  For one smiling day to be free
  To kiss in the sunlight
  And say to the sky:
  "Behold and believe what you see!"
  Behold how my lover loves me!"
    (*He speaks:*)
Tuptim, when can we meet? When?

TUPTIM

It is not possible. We cannot meet alone ever—not ever.
    (LADY THIANG *enters at the back, sees the two lovers together, and goes off, unseen by them.*)

LUN THA
(*As* TUPTIM *suddenly breaks away*)

What is it?

TUPTIM

Someone was here!

(*She looks around fearfully*)
I had a feeling someone was watching us . . . Please go! Please!
(*He leaves.* TUPTIM *sings sadly:*)
To kiss in the sunlight
And say to the sky:
"Behold and believe what you see!
Behold how my lover loves me!"

INTERMEDIATE SCENE

The Palace corridor.

LOUIS *and* CHULALONGKORN *enter from opposite sides. After passing each other in unfriendly silence, each repents and turns at about the same time. Then with a common impulse, they rush toward each other and shake hands.*

CHULALONGKORN

I am sorry we nearly fought just now.

LOUIS

I am too.

CHULALONGKORN

Are you really going away?

LOUIS

Mother plans to leave on the next sailing.

CHULALONGKORN

I am not sure my father will allow your mother to go.

LOUIS

I am not sure whether my mother will allow your father not to allow her to go.

CHULALONGKORN

Why does not your mother admit that she was wrong?

LOUIS

I don't believe that Mother thinks she was wrong.

CHULALONGKORN

It begins to look as if people do not know when they are right or wrong—even after they have grown up.

LOUIS

I have noticed that, too.

CHULALONGKORN

A puzzlement! . . . When I left my father a little while ago, I heard him talking to himself. (*He shakes his head*) He seemed uncertain about many things.

LOUIS

I don't believe grownups are ever certain—they only talk as if they are certain.

CHULALONGKORN
(*Singing:*)
There are times I almost think
They are not sure of what they absolutely know.

LOUIS

I believe they are confused
About conclusions they concluded long ago.

CHULALONGKORN

If my father and your mother are not sure of what they
    absolutely know,
Can you tell me why they fight?

LOUIS

They fight to prove that what they do not know is so!

CHULALONGKORN
(*With the mannerisms of his father*)
Oh-h-h-h-h-h!
Sometimes I think that people going mad.

LOUIS
Ah-h-h-h-h-h!
Sometimes I think that people not so bad.

CHULALONGKORN
But no matter what I think,
I must go on living life
And some day as a leader I must go forth,
Be father to my children
And husband to each wife.
Etcetera, etcetera, and so forth.
    (*His eyes and arms uplifted*)
If my Lord in Heaven, Buddha, show the way,
Every day I try to live another day,
If my Lord in Heaven, Buddha, show the way,
Every day I do my best—for one more day.
But—

LOUIS
Is a puzzlement.
    (*The two boys walk off together thoughtfully.*)

SCENE 5

ANNA's *bedroom.*

    ANNA *is sitting on the bed. She has started to undress, but apparently has stopped, engrossed in her thoughts. Her brows knit. She glares at an imaginary adversary. Her nostrils dilate with scorn. Then she starts to let him have it:*

ANNA

Your servant! Your servant!
Indeed I'm not your servant
    (*Although you give me less than servant's pay*)
I'm a free and independent employé . . . employee.
    (*She paces the floor indignantly, then turns back to "him"*)
Because I'm a woman
You think, like every woman,
I have to be a slave or concubine—
You conceited, self-indulgent libertíne—
    (*Again concerning her pronunciation*)
Libertĭne.
    (*Narrowing her eyes vindictively*)
How I wish I'd called him that! Right to his face!
    (*Turning and addressing "him" again*)
Libertine! And while we're on the subject, sire,
There are certain goings on around this place
That I wish to tell you I do not admire:
I do not like polygamy
Or even moderate bigamy
(I realize
That in your eyes
That clearly makes a prig o' me)
But I am from a civilized land called Wales,
Where men like you are kept in country gaols.

In your pursuit of pleasure, you
Have mistresses who treasure you
(They have no ken
Of other men
Beside whom they can measure you)
A flock of sheep, and you the only ram—
No wonder you're the wonder of Siam!

    (At first elated by this sally a frightened, embarrassed look comes
    into her eyes. She speaks:)
I'm rather glad I didn't say that. . . . Not with the women right
there . . . and the children.
    (She sings wistfully:)
  The children, the children,
  I'll not forget the children,
  No matter where I go I'll always see
  Those little faces looking up at me . . .

  At first, when I started to teach,
  They were shy and remained out of reach,
  But lately I've thought
  One or two have been caught
  By a word I have said
  Or a sentence I've read
  And I've heard an occasional question
  That implied, at the least, a suggestion
  That the work I was trying to do
  Was beginning to show with a few . . .

  That Prince Chulalongkorn
  Is very like his father,
  He's stubborn—but inquisitive and smart . . .
    (Sudden tears)

I must leave this place before they break my heart,
I must leave this place before they break my heart!
>   (*She stops, picks up the watch that is on her pillow and looks down at it*)
Goodness! I had no idea it was so late.
>   (*She resumes undressing, but presently she is back at the* KING *again. She becomes motionless and squints her eyes at "him"*)
Shall I tell you what I think of you?
You're spoiled!
You're a conscientious worker
But you're spoiled.
Giving credit where it's due
There is much I like in you
But it's also very true
That you're spoiled!
>   (*She struts up and down, imitating him*)
Everybody's always bowing
To the King,
Everybody has to grovel
To the King.
By your Buddha you are blessed,
By your ladies you're caressed
But the one who loves you best
Is the King!

All this bowing and kowtowing
To remind you of your royalty,
I find a most disgusting exhibition.
I wouldn't ask a Siamese *cat*
To demonstrate his loyalty
By taking that ridiculous position!

How would you like it if you were a man
Playing the part of a toad?
Crawling around on your elbows and knees,
Eating the dust in the road! . . .
Toads! Toads! All of your people are toads!
> (*She sinks to her knees in scornful imitation of the "toads"*)

Yes, Your Majesty; No, Your Majesty.
Tell us how low to go, Your Majesty;
Make some more decrees, Your Majesty,
Don't let us up off our knees, Your Majesty.
Give us a kick, if it please Your Majesty,
Give us a kick if you would, You Majesty—
> (*"Taking" an imaginary kick*)

Oh! That was good, Your Majesty! . . .
> (*She pounds the floor in her temper, then lies down prone, exhausted . . .* THIANG *enters and rings the string of bells by the door twice.* ANNA *does not, at first, respond. Then, only half believing she has heard a ring, she rises on her knees.*)

ANNA

Who is it?

THIANG

Mrs. Anna, it is I, Lady Thiang.

ANNA

At this hour of the night! (*Opening door*) Come in, Lady Thiang.

THIANG

Mrs. Anna, will you go to King?

ANNA

Now? Has he sent for me?

THIANG

No. But he would be glad to see you. He is deeply wounded man. No one has ever spoken to him as you did today in schoolroom.

ANNA

Lady Thiang, no one has ever behaved to *me* as His Majesty did today in the schoolroom.

THIANG

And there is more distressing thing. Our agents in Singapore have found letters to British Government from people whose greedy eyes are on Siam. They describe King as a barbarian, and suggest making Siam a protectorate.

ANNA

That is outrageous! He is many things I do not like, but he is not a barbarian.

THIANG

Then will you help him?

ANNA

You mean—advise him?

THIANG

It must not sound like advice. King cannot take advice. And if you go to him, he will not bring up subject. You must bring it up.

ANNA

I cannot go to him. It's against all my principles. Certainly not without his *having* asked for me.

THIANG

He wish to be new-blood King with Western ideas. But it is hard for him, Mrs. Anna. And there is something else—Princess Tuptim. I do not tell him—for his sake. I deal with this my own way. But for these other things, he need help, Mrs. Anna.

ANNA

He has *you.*

THIANG

I am not equal to his special needs. He could be great man. But he need special help. He need *you.*

ANNA

Lady Thiang, please don't think I am being stubborn. But I simply cannot go to him. I will not.

THIANG

What more can I say to you?
  (*Frustrated, she tries to think of how else to persuade* ANNA.
  Presently she turns back to ANNA *and starts to sing:*)
This is a man who thinks with his heart,
His heart is not always wise.
This is a man who stumbles and falls,
But this is a man who tries.
This is a man you'll forgive and forgive,
And help and protect, as long as you live . . .

He will not always say
What you would have him say,
But now and then he'll say
Something wonderful.
The thoughtless things he'll do

Will hurt and worry you—
Then all at once he'll do
Something wonderful.
He has a thousand dreams
That won't come true.
You know that he believes in them
And that's enough for you.
You'll always go along,
Defend him when he's wrong
And tell him, when he's strong
He is wonderful.
He'll always need your love—
And so he'll get your love—
A man who needs your love
Can be wonderful!

    (*As she finishes she kneels and looks up at* ANNA *suppliantly.*
ANNA *takes her hand and helps her rise. Then she crosses to the
bed, picks up her jacket and starts to put it on.* THIANG, *taking
this as a sign that her mission is successful, smiles gratefully
and leaves* ANNA *to finish dressing.*)

INTERMEDIATE SCENE

The Palace corridor.
The KRALAHOME *enters and meets* LADY THIANG.

KRALAHOME

Did you succeed? Will she go to him?

THIANG

She will go. She knows he needs her. Tell him.

KRALAHOME

I will tell him she is *anxious* to come. I will tell him it is *she* who needs *him*.

THIANG

That also will be true.
    (*The* KRALAHOME *leaves her.* THIANG *soliloquizes:*)
This woman knows many things, but this, I think, she does not know. . . .
    (*She sings:*)
    She'll always go along,
    Defend him when he's wrong
    And tell him when he's strong
    He is wonderful.
    He'll always need her love
    And so he'll get her love
    A man who needs your love
    Can be wonderful!

SCENE 6

The KING's *study.*

The KING *has been reading a large English Bible, which lies open on the floor beside a cushion arm-rest. There are some English newspapers also on the floor. The* KING *is walking up and down impatiently. He goes up and out to the terrace, looks off left, sees something, and hurries down to the Bible and resumes reading it. Presently,* ANNA *enters on the terrace.*

ANNA
(Making a curtsey)

Your Majesty.

(*She comes into the room*)

Your Majesty.

(*No answer. She looks down over his shoulder*)

Your Majesty is reading the Bible!

KING
(Remaining on the floor)

Mrs. Anna, I think your Moses shall have been a fool.

ANNA

Moses!

KING

Moses! Moses! Moses! I think he shall have been a fool. (*Tapping the Bible*) Here it stands written by him that the world was created in six days. You know and I know it took many ages to create world. I think he shall have been a fool to have written so. What is your opinion?

ANNA

Your Majesty, the Bible was not written by men of science, but
by men of faith. (*The* KING *considers this*) It was their explanation
of the miracle of creation, which is the same miracle—whether
it took six days or many centuries.

KING

(*Rising*)

Hm. (*He is impressed by her explanation but, of course, would not
say so*) You have come to apologize?

ANNA

I am sorry, Your Majesty, but . . .

KING

Good! You apologize.

ANNA

Your Majesty, I . . .

KING

I accept!

ANNA

Your Majesty, nothing that has been said can alter the fact that
in my country, anyone who makes a promise must . . .

KING

Silence! (*Pursuing his own thoughts*) Tell me about President
Lingkong of America. Shall Mr. Lingkong be winning this war
he is fighting at present?

ANNA

No one knows, Your Majesty.

KING

Does he have enough guns and elephants for transporting same?

ANNA

(*Not quite smiling*)

I don't think they have elephants in America, Your Majesty.

KING

No elephants! Then I shall send him some. (*Handing her a notebook and pencil*) Write letter to Mr. Lingkong.

ANNA

Now?

KING

Now! When else! Now is always best time. (*He sits on the floor.*)

ANNA

Very well, Your Majesty.

KING

(*Dictating*)

From Phra Maha Mongut, by the blessing of the highest super agency in the world of the whole Universe, the King of Siam, the Sovereign of all tributary countries adjacent and around in every direction, etcetera, etcetera, etcetera.

(*Almost without a break*)

Do you not have any respect for me?

(ANNA *looks up from her notebook, having no idea what he means*)

Why do you stand over my head? I cannot stand all the time. And in this country, no one's head shall be higher than King's. From now on in presence you shall so conduct yourself like all other subjects.

ANNA

You mean on the floor! I am sorry. I shall try very hard not to let my head be as high as Your Majesty's—but I simply cannot grovel on the floor. I couldn't possibly work that way—or think!

KING
(*He rises and studies her before he speaks*)
You are very difficult woman. But you will observe care that head shall never be higher than mine. If I shall sit, you shall sit. If I shall kneel, you shall kneel, etcetera, etcetera, etcetera.
(*Pause.*)

ANNA

Very well, Your Majesty.

KING

Is promise?

ANNA

Is promise.

KING

Good.
(*He squats down on his heels to resume dictating.* ANNA *sits on the floor nearby*)
To His Royal Presidency of the United States of America, Abra-Hom Lingkong, etcetera . . . you fix up. It has occurred to us . . .

(*He stretches out prone, his chin leaning on his hand. Then he notices that* ANNA's *head is higher*)
It has occurred to us—
(*He gives* ANNA *a significant look, and she reluctantly keeps her promise, lying prone, so that her head is no higher than his*)
It has occurred to us that if several pairs of young male elephants were turned loose in forests of America, after a while they would increase . . .

ANNA
(*Her head snapping up from her dictating*)
Your Majesty—just *male* elephants?

KING
(*Refusing to acknowledge his mistake*)
You put in details! (*He rises, and she does also*) Tonight my mind is on other matters—very important matters.

ANNA
(*Knowing he is getting near the subject he really wants to talk about*)
Anything you want to discuss with me?

KING
Why should I discuss important matters with woman?

ANNA
Very well, Your Majesty. (*She curtseys*) Then I will say good night.

KING
Good night!
(ANNA *goes up toward the terrace, then turns, to give him another chance.*)

ANNA

Your Majesty . . .

KING
(*Relieved and eager*)

What, what, what?

ANNA
(*To cue him*)

I was wondering—When the boat arrived from Singapore yesterday . . .

KING

Singapore! Ha!

ANNA

Was there any news from abroad?

KING

News! Yes, there are news! They call me barbarian.

ANNA

Who?

KING

Certain parties who would use this as excuse to steal my country. Suppose you were Queen Victoria and somebody tell you King of Siam is barbarian. Do you believe?

ANNA

Well, Your Majesty . . .

KING

You will! You will! You will! You will believe I am barbarian because there is no one to speak otherwise.

ANNA

But this is a lie!

KING

It is a *false* lie!

ANNA

What have you decided to do about it?

KING

(*After a pause*)

You guess!

ANNA

Well, if someone were sending a big lie about me to England, I should do my best to send the truth to England . . . Is that what you have decided to do, Your Majesty?

KING

Yes. That is what I have decided to do. (*To himself*) But how? (*He crosses to her*) Guess how I shall do this!

ANNA

Well, my guess would be that when Sir Edward Ramsay arrives here . . .

KING

Ramsay? Ramsay?

ANNA

The British diplomat.

KING

Ah, yes—on way from Singapore.

ANNA

We wrote to him last month.

KING

When he is here, I shall take opportunity of expressing my opinion of English thieves who wish to steal Siam. I shall show him who is barbarian! (*Noticing her disapproval*) What is this face you put on?

ANNA

Well, Your Majesty, my guess is that you will not fight with Sir Edward.

KING

I will not?

ANNA

No, Your Majesty. You will entertain him and his party in an especially grand manner. In this way you will make them all witnesses in your favor. They will return to England and report to the Queen that you are not a barbarian.

KING

Naturally . . . naturally! (*He paces up and down, delighted with the solution*) This is what I shall have intended to do.

ANNA

This is the only way to get the better of the British. Stand up to them. Put your best foot forward.
(*The* KING, *bewildered, holds up his foot and looks at it*)
That is an expression, Your Majesty. It means dress up in your best clothes. Show them your most intelligent men, your most beautiful women. Edward admires beautiful women.

KING
(*Suspiciously*)

Edward? You call him this?

ANNA

We are old friends. I knew him in Bombay before I was married.

KING

Ah! . . . (*Walking past her thoughtfully*) Shall it be proper for the British dignitary to see my women with no shoes on their feet? Shall it be proper for them to put their best *bare* feet forward? No! Sir Ramsay will go back and tell Queen I am a barbarian. Why do *you* not think of this?

ANNA
(*Suddenly inspired*)

We shall dress them up European fashion.

KING

You mean dress them in . . . dresses?
(ANNA *nods. They both become increasingly excited.*)

ANNA

How many women can I have to sew for me?

KING

All women in Kingdom. How many dresses?

ANNA

That depends on how many ladies are chosen by Your Majesty.

KING

You shall tell me which of my women are most like Europeans,
for dressing like same.
  (*He crosses quickly to the throne-table, strikes a gong and shouts*)
Wake up! Wake up, everybody! Wives! Etcetera, etcetera, etcetera!
  (*He returns to* ANNA)
I shall command Chinese artists to paint their faces very pale.
And you shall educate them in European custom and manners
for presentation.

ANNA

I wonder how much time we shall have.

KING

Sir Ramsay's gunboat last reported off Songkla. How long he
take depend on how many ports he call into. Let us say we have
one week.

ANNA

One week! But, Your Majesty, I don't think . . . one week!

KING

In this time whole world was created—*Moses* say! . . . Are there
any details I do not think of so far?

ANNA

You must give them a fine dinner—a European dinner.

KING

I was going to.

ANNA

And a ball. With music.

KING

Music. (*His face lights up*) And dancing!

ANNA

That's right! Dancing!

KING

Why do *you* not think of dancing?

ANNA

It was an inspired idea, Your Majesty.
(*Now, in answer to the gong, the wives enter in nightdress.*
TUPTIM *is first.* THIANG *also enters, but not in nightdress*)
We can give them a theatrical performance. Tuptim has written
a play, a version of *Uncle Tom's Cabin.*

KING

Ha! We shall give them theatrical performance. We shall show
them who is barbarian!
(*To the wives*)
Line up! Line up! Line up!
(*They do so*)
Lady Thiang! On Saturday next, at nine o'clock post meridian,
we shall give fine dinner—European dinner, for probably thirty
people.
(THIANG *bows*)

You are to instruct steward during week he shall make eminent European dishes for tasting. I shall taste and schoolteacher shall taste.

> (*The children begin coming in, accompanied by their nurses and the Amazons. They rub their eyes and yawn. The* KING *turns to* ANNA)

You say who is most like European lady for dressing like same.

> (ANNA *crosses to inspect the wives. The* KING *continues his order to* THIANG)

You are to make tablecloth of finest white silk for very long table. Also instruct court musicians to learn music of Europe for dancing, etcetera.

> (*The* TWINS, *coming in, have gone around him and are now in front of him*)

What? What? What? Am I to be annoyed by children at this moment?

> (*A* NURSE, *having lost her charge, comes running around him, clapping her hands*)

Who? Who? Who?

> (*All drop to the floor at his angry tones. Then the object of the* NURSE'S *solicitude, a very tiny boy, crawls between the* KING's *legs and crouches in front of him*)

Mrs. Anna, we must be more scientific with children!

> (*He walks up and down angrily*)

For the next week, the men and women of my kingdom will work without sleeping until all is ready, and for what is not done, each man and woman shall be beaten a hundred strokes. Everyone must know this, Lady Thiang. Tell this to everyone! Above all, I must not be worried by anything . . .

> (*There is a tremendous report that sounds like a cannon, and fireworks appear on the backdrop. Discipline is immediately abandoned, and there are shrieks and cries of fear. The children*

huddle together with the nurses and Amazons. The KING *and* ANNA *run up to the terrace)*
What can this be?
(*Another terrifying report.*)

ANNA
(*Pointing to the fireworks*)
Look, Your Majesty!

KING

Fireworks!
(*The children, reassured, move forward a bit to enjoy the show*)
Fireworks at this hour in the morning! No one may order fireworks but me.

KRALAHOME
(*Rushing in*)
Your Majesty—the British! The gunboat!

KING

They attack?

KRALAHOME

No! They salute, and we answer with fireworks. It is Sir Edward Ramsay and his party.

ANNA
(*Horrified*)
Now?

KRALAHOME

Now! They must have come direct from Songkla. No stops.

ANNA

No stops!

KING

Tell them to go back! We are not ready!

KRALAHOME

Not ready, Your Majesty?

KING

You do not know, you do not know. I had planned best idea I ever get.

ANNA

We can still do it, Your Majesty—*you* can do it.

KING

Ha! When English arrive we will put them to bed. Tomorrow morning we shall send them on sightseeing trip.

ANNA

We shall start now, this minute. Work! Work! We have only eighteen hours, but I shall do it somehow!

KING
(*Sternly*)
I shall do it. You shall help me.
(*Resuming his orders, energetically*)
No one shall sleep tonight or tomorrow. We shall work even when the sun shines in the middle of the day. We shall . . .
(*He sees a group of priests passing on the terrace*)
Ah! Priests!
(*He motions them to come in*)

First we shall ask help from Buddha. Bow to him! Bow! Bow! Bow!
(*They all sink to their knees, the* KING *included, and raise their hands in prayerful attitude.* ANNA *remains standing but bows her head. The* KING *chants:*)
Oh, Buddha, give us the aid of your strength and your wisdom.

ALL
(*Repeating chant*)
Oh, Buddha, give us the aid of your strength and your wisdom.
(*The* KING *sits back on his heels.*)

KING
(*Clapping his hands as Orientals do to get Buddha's attention*)
And help us to prove to the visiting English that we are extraordinary and remarkable people.

ALL
And help us to prove to the visiting English that we are extraordinary and remarkable people.
(*During the repetition, the* KING *leans forward and down in a crouch, and steals a glance at* ANNA.)

KING
Help also Mrs. Anna to keep awake for scientific sewing of dresses, even though she be only a woman and a Christian, and therefore unworthy of your interest.
(ANNA *looks up in surprise at the mention of her name, and comes to the* KING *in protest.*)

ALL
Help also Mrs. Anna to keep awake for scientific sewing of dresses, even though she be only a woman and a Christian, and therefore unworthy of your interest.

KING

(During the repetition of the prayer, to ANNA*)*

A promise is a promise! Your head cannot be higher than mine! A promise!

(Reluctantly, she sinks to a kneeling position to match his. The orchestra plays strains of "Something Wonderful")

And, Buddha, I promise you I shall give this unworthy woman a house—a house of her own—a brick residence adjoining the royal palace, according to agreement, etcetera, etcetera, etcetera.

ALL

And, Buddha, I promise you I shall give this unworthy woman a house—a house of her own—a brick residence adjoining the royal palace, according to agreement, etcetera, etcetera, etcetera.

(As they repeat his words, the KING *watching to make sure that* ANNA *imitates him, sits back on his heels, then leans forward, finally stretching out, prone. They are both flat on their faces. Then he raises his head and rests his chin on his hand. She does the same. Fireworks burst through the air beyond the terrace.* ANNA *and the* KING *regard each other warily. Who is taming whom?)*

Curtain

ACT 2

Yul Brynner and Deborah Kerr in the film version, 1956.

The original Broadway marquee at the St. James Theatre, 1951.

Yul Brynner and Gertrude Lawrence in the original Broadway production, 1951.

"The Small House of Uncle Thomas," 1956 film.

"The Small House of Uncle Thomas," 2015 Lincoln Center Theater production at the Vivian Beaumont Theater.

Set design rendering by Jo Mielziner for the original 1951 Broadway production.

Set design by Brian Thomson for the Australian production in 1991. The production played on Broadway in 1996 and later toured the U.S.

Yul Brynner and Constance Towers, 1977 Broadway revival.

Yul Brynner and Mary Beth Peil, 1985 Broadway revival. Brynner's final performances.

Celeste Holm, original Broadway production. Summer of 1952, during Gertrude Lawrence's vacation.

Jason Scott and Angela Lansbury, 1977 Broadway revival, during Yul Brynner's vacation.

Lou Diamond Phillips and Donna Murphy, 1996 Broadway revival.

Hayley Mills and Tony Marinyo, 1991 Australian revival. Mills later toured with the production in the U.S.

Lou Diamond Phillips and Faith Prince, 1996 Broadway revival. (Prince followed Donna Murphy.)

Marie Osmond and Kevin Gray, 1996 Broadway revival. (Later in the run.)

Elaine Stritch and Renato Cibelli, 1965.

Farley Granger and Barbara Cook, 1960 New York City Center Light Opera revival.

Kelli O'Hara and Ken Watanabe, 2015 Lincoln Center Theater production at the Vivian Beaumont Theater.

Daniel Dae Kim and Marin Mazzie, 2015 Lincoln Center Theater production at the Vivian Beaumont Theater. (Later in the run.)

Yul Brynner and Gertrude Lawrence, 1951 original Broadway production.
Backstage between shows on a two-show day.

SCENE 1

The schoolroom.

It has been converted into a dressing room for tonight. The floor and tables are littered with dressmaking materials. The wives are all dressed in their new hoopskirts, mostly finished, but all are uncomfortable in the unaccustomed clothes. A Chinese artist is painting the face of one. Others are receiving last-minute touches from two seamstresses. The faces of the wives are powdered white.

LADY THIANG *enters. She has on a Western bodice and a penang.*

THIANG

Ladies! Ladies! Clear everything away! Quickly now!
(The wives and seamstresses clear away the materials.)

A WIFE

Lady Thiang, what is this costume? (*Pointing to penang*) Here is East— (*Pointing to bodice*) Here is West!

THIANG

Have too much work to do! Cannot move fast in swollen skirt.

ANOTHER WIFE

Lady Thiang, why must we dress like this for British?

THIANG

Whatever Mrs. Anna want us to do is wise and good, but this— (*Indicating hoopskirts*) is a puzzlement.
(She sings:)

To prove we're not barbarians
They dress us up like savages!
To prove we're not barbarians
We wear a funny skirt!

WIVES

To prove we're not barbarians
They dress us up like savages!
To prove we're not barbarians
We wear a funny skirt!

THIANG

Western people funny,
Western people funny,
Western people funny,
Of that there is no doubt.
They feel so sentimental
About the Oriental,
They always try to turn us
Inside down and upside out!

WIVES

Upside out and inside down!

THIANG

To bruise and pinch our little toes
Our feet are cramped in leather shoes—
They'd break if we had brittle toes,
But now they only hurt!

WIVES

To bruise and pinch our little toes
Our feet are cramped in leather shoes—

They'd break if we had brittle toes,
But now they only hurt!

Western people funny,
Western people funny,
Western people funny,
Too funny to be true!

THIANG

They think they civilize us
Whenever they advise us
To learn to make the same mistake
That they are making too!

ALL

They think they civilize us
Whenever they advise us
To learn to make the same mistake
That they are making too!

They make quite a few!

ANNA
(*Entering*)
Lady Thiang, here are the napkins for dinner. Will you put them
on the table?

THIANG
(*Taking them*)
Thank you.

ANNA

Thank *you*.

(LADY THIANG *goes out*)
Now, ladies, turn around and let me see how you look.
(*The* WIVES *spread out and turn so that* ANNA *can see their backs. The* KING *enters. They immediately prostrate themselves, the hoops flying up behind them.* ANNA *sees the horrid truth*)
Oh, my goodness gracious!

KING

What shall be trouble now?

ANNA

I forgot! They have practically no—undergarments!

KING

Undergarments! (*He claps his hands and the* WIVES *rise*) Of what importance are undergarments at this time?

ANNA
(*Stiffly*)

Of great importance.

KING

Are *you* wearing undergarments?

ANNA

Of course, Your Majesty!

KING
(*Pointing to hoopskirt, derisively*)

That a woman has no legs is useless to pretend. Wherefore, then, swollen skirt?

ANNA

The wide skirt is symbolic. It is the circle within which a female is protected.

KING

This is necessary? Englishmen are so aggressive? I did not know.

ANNA
(*Going to the* SEAMSTRESSES, *who help her remove her smock*)
I said it was symbolic.

KING

These undergarments—they are devised in symbolic, elaborate and ornamental manner?

ANNA

Sometimes.
(*Her gown now revealed, the* WIVES *gasp their admiration.*)

KING
(*Looking at her bare shoulders*)
This is what you are going to wear?

ANNA

Why, yes. Do you like it?

KING

This is what all the other visiting ladies shall look like?

ANNA

Most of them . . . I believe.

KING

You are certain this is customary? (*Indicating her bare shoulders*)
Etcetera, etcetera, etcetera . . .

ANNA

Yes, I am certain it is customary. What is so extraordinary about
bare shoulders? Your own ladies . . .

KING

Ah, yes. But is different! They do not wear so many coverings up
on other parts of body, etcetera, etcetera, and therefore . . .

ANNA
(*Irritated, like any woman who, displaying a new dress,
meets unexpected criticism*)
Therefore what?

KING

Is different.

ANNA

I am sorry His Majesty does not approve.

KING

I do not say I do not approve, but I do say . . .

PHRA ALACK
(*Entering, prostrating himself*)
The English—they are in palace.
(*This causes immediate confusion among the wives who huddle
in a frightened group.*)

THARA

They will eat us!

ANNA

They will do nothing of the kind!

KING

(*Calling* ANNA *to him, he gives her a piece of paper*)
Herewith shall be list of subjects you shall try to bring up for
talk. On such subjects I am very brilliant, and will make great
impression. You begin with Moses.

ANNA

(*Taking the paper and crowding in some
last-minute coaching*)
Now remember, Your Majesty—Courtwright is the editor of a
newspaper in Singapore . . .
(*She is interrupted by the entrance of* SIR EDWARD RAMSAY,
*who has wandered into the room by mistake. One wife screams
in fright.*)

ANOTHER WIFE

(*Indicating* SIR EDWARD'*s monocle*)
Oh, evil eye! Evil eye!
(*The wives in an uncontrollable stampede throw their hoop-
skirts over their heads and rush out. From the look on* SIR
EDWARD'*s face, it is clear that they should have been supplied
with undergarments.*)

ANNA

Ladies! Ladies! Come back! Don't! Come back! Oh, dear! Edward!
Oh, Your Majesty, this is dreadful!

KING
(*Furious*)
Why have you not educated these girls in English custom of spying glass?

SIR EDWARD
Ah, my monocle. Was that what frightened them? Hello, Anna, my dear.

KING
(*Before they can complete their handshake*)
Who? Who? Who?

ANNA
Your Majesty, may I present Sir Edward Ramsay?

SIR EDWARD
(*Bowing*)
Your Majesty. (*He turns to* ANNA) How are you, Anna?

KING
I regret, sir, my ladies have not given good impression.

SIR EDWARD
On the contrary, Your Majesty, I have never received so good an impression in so short a time. You have most attractive pupils, Anna.
(*The* KING *is clearly annoyed by the intimacy between* ANNA *and* SIR EDWARD.)

ANNA
Tomorrow you must meet my younger pupils—His Majesty's children. They are making wonderful progress.

SIR EDWARD

I shall be delighted. (*To* KING) How many children have you, Your Majesty?

KING

Seventy-seven now, but I am not married very long. Next month expecting three more.

SIR EDWARD

No problem at all about an heir to the throne, is there?
  (*This sally falls flat with the* KING, *so he turns to* ANNA, *but it doesn't amuse her either*)
I—er—I suppose I should apologize for wandering into this room. The rest of the party were ahead of me and . . .

ANNA

I'm so glad you decided to visit us—to visit His Majesty I mean, of course . . .

SIR EDWARD

It was your postscript to His Majesty's letter that . . .

KING
(*Turning with alert suspicion*)

Postscript?

ANNA

His Majesty was most happy when you decided to accept his invitation . . . Weren't you, Your Majesty?

KING
(*Trying to figure it out*)

I was . . . happy.

KRALAHOME
(*Entering*)
Your Majesty, dinner is about to be served, and I would first like
to present your guests to you in the reception room.

KING
(*Clapping his hands happily, and going off*)
Dinner, dinner, dinner!

ANNA
(*To* KRALAHOME)
You have met?

KRALAHOME
(*Bowing*)
Your Excellency. (*He goes off. A waltz is being played off-stage.*)

SIR EDWARD
Anna, my dear, you're looking lovelier than ever.

ANNA
Thank you, Edward.

SIR EDWARD
Found a job to do, eh? People you can help, that's it, isn't it?
Extraordinary how one gets attached to people who need one.
(*Listening*) Do you hear that? Do you know we danced to that
once? (*She nods*) Bombay. Still dance?

ANNA
Not very often.

SIR EDWARD

You should. (*He puts his arm around her waist and they dance.*)

ANNA

Edward, I think we'd better . . .

SIR EDWARD

Are you sure you don't ever get homesick?

ANNA

No, Edward. I told you, I have nothing there—no one.
(*The* KING *enters and watches them.*)

EDWARD

Anna, do you remember that I once asked you to marry me—
before Tom came along?

ANNA

Dear Edward . . .

KING

(*Interrupting, furiously*)

Dancing—*after* dinner!

SIR EDWARD

Oh, sorry, sir. I'm afraid I started talking over old times.

KING

(*Looking sternly at* ANNA)

It was my impression Mrs. Anna would be of help for seating of
guests at dinner table, etcetera, etcetera, etcetera.

SIR EDWARD

In that case, we'd better be going in, Anna. (*He moves toward her, offering his arm.*)

KING

(*Coming between them, offering his arm*)
Yes, better be going in . . . Anna.
(*She takes the* KING's *arm, and they start off left,* SIR EDWARD *following.*)

ANNA

(*After a quick look at the paper the* KING *has given her*)
His Majesty made an interesting point about Moses the other day when he was reading the Bible. It seems he takes issue with the statement that . . .
(*They are off.*)

SCENE 2

The Palace grounds.

  TUPTIM *enters and crosses the stage, looking back furtively. She starts guiltily as she sees* LADY THIANG.

THIANG

Princess Tuptim, dinner is over. King and his English guests are on way to theater pavilion. Should you not be there to begin your play?

TUPTIM
(*Rattled*)

I came out here to memorize my lines.

THIANG
(*Stopping her as she starts to go*)

I think not, Princess. I have seen you and Lun Tha together. I do not tell King this. For *his* sake. I do not wish to hurt him. But your lover will leave Siam tonight.

TUPTIM

Tonight?

THIANG

Now go to the theater, Princess.

  (TUPTIM *exits.* THIANG *starts off, stops as she sees* LUN THA *enter left, looks at him with stern suspicion, then exits.* LUN THA *crosses to the other side, and calls off, in a whisper.*)

LUN THA

Tuptim!

TUPTIM
(*Entering*)

Turn back and look the other way. (LUN THA *instantly does so*) I am here in the shadow of the wall. I will stay here until she turns the corner. . . . She has told me you will leave Siam tonight, but I don't believe her.

LUN THA

It is true, Tuptim. They have ordered me onto the first ship that leaves for Burma, and it is tonight.

TUPTIM
(*Running to him*)

What will we do?

LUN THA

You are coming with me!

TUPTIM

I!

LUN THA

You have been a slave long enough! Secret police will all be at the theater. Meet me here, after your play. Everything is arranged.

TUPTIM

I cannot believe it.

LUN THA

I can. It will be just as I have pictured it a million times.
(*He sings:*)
    I have dreamed that your arms are lovely,
    I have dreamed what a joy you'll be.

I have dreamed every word you'll whisper
When you're close,
Close to me.
How you look in the glow of evening
I have dreamed, and enjoyed the view.
In these dreams I've loved you so
That by now I think I know
What it's like to be loved by you—
I will love being loved by you.

TUPTIM

Alone and awake I've looked at the stars,
The same that smiled on you;
And time and again I've thought all the things
That you were thinking too.

I have dreamed that your arms are lovely,
I have dreamed what a joy you'll be.
I have dreamed every word you'll whisper
When you're close,
Close to me.
How you look in the glow of evening
I have dreamed, and enjoyed the view.
In these dreams I've loved you so
That by now I think I know

TUPTIM AND LUN THA

What it's like to be loved by you—
I will love being loved by you.
(ANNA *enters.* TUPTIM *runs to her.*)

TUPTIM

Mrs. Anna!

ANNA

Tuptim, they are looking for you at the theater. I guessed you were both here. I ran out to warn you. I do think you're being rather reckless.

TUPTIM

Yes, I will go.
(*She starts away, then turns back and surprises* ANNA *with a suddenly serious tone in her voice*)
I must say good-bye to you now, Mrs. Anna.
(*She kneels, kisses* ANNA'*s hand impulsively, and runs off.*)

ANNA
(*To* LUN THA)

Gracious! Anyone would think that she never expected to see me again.
(*He looks at her steadily, and catching his look, she crosses him, looking after* TUPTIM.)

LUN THA

Mrs. Anna, we are leaving tonight.

ANNA

Leaving? How?

LUN THA

Don't ask me how. It is better if you don't know. We shall never forget you, Mrs. Anna. (*He kisses her hand*) Never.

ANNA
(*As she goes*)

God bless you both!
(*Alone, thoughtfully, she sings:*)

I know how it feels to have wings on your heels
And to fly down a street in a trance.
You fly down a street on the chance that you'll meet,
And you meet—not really by chance.
Don't cry, young lovers, whatever you do,
Don't cry because I'm alone.
All of my memories are happy tonight,
I've had a love of my own.
I've had a love of my own, like yours,
I've had a love of my own.
   (*She starts off as the curtain closes.*)

SCENE 3

The theater pavilion.
  Ballet: "The Small House of Uncle Thomas."
  Before a curtain two attendants carry on a drum and a gong.
The drummer takes his place. The royal singers enter ceremoniously
and take their places at the opposite corner. TUPTIM *enters and stands*
in front of the singers.
  The curtain opens, revealing the royal dancers dressed in traditional
costumes, their faces painted chalk-white.

TUPTIM
(*Speaking straight out at the audience, as if addressing*
the KING *and his British visitors*)
Your Majesty, and honorable guests, I beg to put before you
"Small House of Uncle Thomas."
  (*A tiny cabin is brought on.*)

CHORUS
Small house of Uncle Thomas!
Small house of Uncle Thomas!
Written by a woman,
Harriet Beecher Stow-a!

TUPTIM
House is in Kingdom of Kentucky, ruled by most wicked King
in all America—Simon of Legree.
  (*The gong is struck. The dancers make a traditional gesture*
  denoting terror)
Your Majesty, I beg to put before you loving friends . . . Uncle
Thomas!
  (*He enters from cabin.*)

CHORUS

Dear old Uncle Thomas.

TUPTIM

Little Eva.
(*She enters from cabin.*)

CHORUS

Blessed Little Eva.

TUPTIM

Little Topsy.
(*She enters from cabin.*)

CHORUS

Mischief-maker, Topsy.

TUPTIM

Happy people.

CHORUS

Very happy people.
(*The happy people dance.*)

TUPTIM

Happy people. Happy people.
(*The dance over,* TUPTIM *continues*)
Your Majesty, I beg to put before you one who is not happy—
the slave, Eliza.
(ELIZA *enters from cabin.*)

CHORUS

Poor Eliza, poor Eliza,
Poor unfortunate slave.

TUPTIM

Eliza's lord and master
King Simon of Legree.
She hates her lord and master.
   (*The gong and cymbal combine in a frightening crash, and the
   dancers again pantomime terror according to the traditional
   gesture*)
And fears him.
   (*Gong and cymbal again*)
This King has sold her lover
To far away province of O-hee-o
Lover's name is George.

CHORUS

George.

TUPTIM

Baby in her arms
Also called George.

CHORUS

George.
   (ELIZA *enacts what* TUPTIM *describes.*)

TUPTIM

Eliza say she run away and look for her lover George.

CHORUS

George.

TUPTIM

So she bid good-bye to friends and start on her escape. "The escape."

(ELIZA *now dances and mines "the escape."*)

CHORUS

Run, Eliza, run, Eliza!
Run from Simon.

TUPTIM

Poor Eliza running,
And run into a rainstorm.
   (*The rainstorm is depicted by dancers waving scarves. After the "storm" is over,* ELIZA *gives her "baby" a shake to dry it off*)
Comes a mountain.
   (*The mountain is formed by three men.*)

CHORUS

Climb, Eliza!
   (*After climbing the "mountain"* ELIZA *rubs her feet.*)

TUPTIM

Hide, Eliza!

CHORUS

Hide, Eliza, hide from Simon!
Hide in forest.
   (*The trees of the forest are dancers holding branches.*)

TUPTIM

Eliza very tired.
   (ELIZA *exits wearily*)
Your Majesty, I regret to put before you King Simon of Legree.

(SIMON, *wearing a terrible, three-headed masque, is borne on
by attendants. His slaves prostrate themselves before him in
the manner of the subjects of the King of Siam.*)

CHORUS

Because one slave has run away
Simon beating every slave.
  (SIMON *dances down an aisle of quivering slaves, slashing at
  them with his huge sword.*)

TUPTIM

Simon clever man. He decide to hunt Eliza, not only with soldiers,
but with scientific dogs who sniff and smell, and thereby discover
all who run away from King.
  (*Now the chase ensues. Dancers with the dog masques portray
  bloodhounds who "sniff and smell" and pick up poor* ELIZA's
  scent. ELIZA *runs from one side of the stage to the other always
  followed by the dogs, and by more of the* KING's *men in each
  episode, and finally by the horrible* SIMON *himself. And the
  pursuers keep getting closer to her.*)

CHORUS

Run, Eliza, run!
Run, Eliza, run!

Run, Eliza, run, run.
Run from Simon, run, run!

Eliza run,
Eliza run from Simon, run!
Eliza run,
Eliza run from Simon, run!

Eliza run,
Eliza run,
Run, run!

Simon getting closer . . .
Eliza getting tired . . .
Run, Eliza,
Run from Simon,
Run, Eliza, run!

TUPTIM

Eliza come to river,
Eliza come to river.
> (*Two dancers run on with a long strip of silk which they wave to indicate a flowing river.* ELIZA *stands before the "river" in frustrated horror.*)

CHORUS

Poor Eliza!

TUPTIM

Who can save Eliza?

CHORUS

Only Buddha,
Buddha, Buddha, Buddha!
Save her, Buddha,
Save her, Buddha, save her! . . .
What will Buddha do?
> (*Gong. The curtains part at back revealing Buddha on a high throne.*)

TUPTIM

Buddha make a miracle!

(*An angel with golden wings enters*)

Buddha send an angel down.

Angel make the wind blow cold.

(*The* ANGEL *blows on the "river" through a golden horn. The strip of silk, indicating the "river," is made to lie flat on the stage. It no longer ripples. The "river" is frozen!*)

Make the river water hard,

Hard enough to walk upon.

CHORUS

Buddha make a miracle!

Praise to Buddha!

(ELIZA *looks down at the river, somewhat puzzled. The* ANGEL *puts away her horn, then joins* ELIZA, *takes her hand and proceeds to teach her how to slide on a frozen river.*)

TUPTIM

Angel show her how to walk on frozen water.

(ELIZA *and the* ANGEL *now do a pas-de-deux in the manner of two skaters.* ELIZA *picks it up quickly and seems to like it*)

Now, as token of his love,

Buddha make a new miracle.

(*As* TUPTIM *describes this new miracle, the* CHORUS *keeps singing:*)

CHORUS

Praise to Buddha!

Praise to Buddha!

TUPTIM

Send from heaven stars and blossoms,
Look like lace upon the sky.
    (*Several men enter with long poles like fishing rods, and from
    the lines dangle large representations of snowflakes*)
So Eliza cross the river,
Hidden by this veil of lace.
    (TUPTIM *steps down a few feet*)
Forgot to tell you name of miracle—snow!
    (*Suddenly* ELIZA *looks terrified, and no wonder!*)

TUPTIM AND CHORUS

Of a sudden she can see
Wicked Simon of Legree,
Sliding 'cross the river fast,
With his bloodhounds and his slaves!
    (*Now* SIMON *and his slaves enter and* ELIZA *runs away. The*
    ANGEL, *too, has disappeared at the wrong moment. Now,*
    while SIMON *and his followers start to slide and skate on the*
    "river," very much as ELIZA *had, the "river" begins to be active*
    again. The strip of silk is made to wave, and the two men
    carrying it lift it up and start to envelop SIMON *and his party*
    in its folds.)

TUPTIM

What has happened to the river?

TUPTIM AND CHORUS

Buddha has called out the sun,
Sun has made the water soft.
Wicked Simon and his slaves
Fall in river and are drowned.

(*This is true. The* ANGEL *has come back with a huge sun, which he holds and directs upon the river. The silk is wrapped around* SIMON *and his party, and they are dragged off in it, drowned as they can be.*)

TUPTIM

On other side of river is pretty city, Canada, where Eliza sees lovely small house—guess who live in house? (*A replica of the first cabin is brought on, but this one has snow on the roof and ice on the windowpanes*) Uncle Thomas.
(*He enters as before.*)

CHORUS

Dear old Uncle Thomas.

TUPTIM

Little Eva.
(*She enters.*)

CHORUS

Blessed Little Eva.

TUPTIM

Little Topsy.
(*She enters.*)

CHORUS

Mischief-maker, Topsy.

TUPTIM

Lover George.
(*The* ANGEL *enters, but this time without wings.*)

CHORUS

Faithful lover George.

TUPTIM

Who is looking like angel to Eliza.
 (*A chord is struck*)
They have all escaped from
Wicked King and make happy reunion.
 (*They do a brief dance*)
Topsy glad that Simon die,
Topsy dance for joy.
 (*She dances a few steps, then strikes a pose*)
I tell you what Harriet Beecher Stowe say
That Topsy say:
 (*Cymbal crash*)
"I specks I'se de wickedest critter
In de world!"
 (*Another cymbal crash.* TUPTIM *frowns, an earnest, dramatic
 note comes into her voice. She steps forward*)
But I do not believe
Topsy is a wicked critter.
Because I too am glad
For death of King.
Of any King who pursues
Slave who is unhappy and tries to join her lover!
 (*The dancers look frightened.* TUPTIM's *emotions are running
 away with her*)
And, Your Majesty, I wish to say to you . . .
Your Majesty—
 (*A chord is struck.* TUPTIM *collects herself*)
And honorable guests . . .
I will tell you the end of story . . .

(*The dancers look relieved. She is back in the make-believe tale of "Uncle Thomas."*)
Is very sad ending.
Buddha has saved Eliza
But with the blessings of Buddha
Also comes sacrifice.
(*Gong. Buddha is again revealed.*)

CHORUS

Poor Little Eva,
Poor Little Eva,
Poor unfortunate child.
(EVA *comes to center, weeping.*)

TUPTIM

Is Buddha's wish
That Eva come to him
And thank him personally
For saving of Eliza and baby.
And so she die
And go to arms of Buddha.
(EVA, *bowing her sad adieux to the audience, turns and climbs the steps to Buddha's high throne.*)

CHORUS

Praise to Buddha,
Praise to Buddha!
(*The music mounts in a loud and uplifting crescendo. The curtain closes on the tragic tableau. The singers and dancers perform ceremonious bows in front of the curtain.*)

SCENE 4

The KING'*s study.*

ANNA *is seated on a pile of books beside the throne-table. The* KING *is walking up and down, smoking a long cigar.* SIR EDWARD *is standing, center, and the* KRALAHOME *is in the shadows to his left. It is night, after the banquet.*

SIR EDWARD

The evening was a great success, Your Majesty. I enjoyed Princess Tuptim's play immensely.

KING

This play did not succeed with me. It is immoral for King to drown when pursuing slave who deceive him. (*Pacing angrily*) Immoral! Immoral! Tuptim shall know of my displeasure.

SIR EDWARD

Your conversation at dinner was most amusing.

KING

I was forced to laugh myself. I was so funny.

SIR EDWARD

Her Majesty, Queen Victoria, will be very glad to know that we have come to such "felicity of agreement" about Siam.

KING

And very happy I am thereof. Very happy.

SIR EDWARD

I think now, with your permission, I should take my leave.
(*He bows. The* KING *extends his hand in a manner clearly*

showing how unfamiliar he is with this Western amenity. SIR
EDWARD *shakes his hand, then bows to* ANNA)
Good-bye, Anna, my dear. It was lovely to see you again.

ANNA

Good-bye, Edward.
  (*He goes out, escorted by the* KRALAHOME. *The* KING *turns to*
  ANNA)
Well, Your Majesty . . .

KING

It is all over. (*He puts his cigar in a bowl, very glad to be rid of it.*)

ANNA

May I remove my shawl? It is a very hot night.
  (*She does so. This makes the* KING *vaguely uneasy. He closes
  his own jacket across his bare chest as if to compensate for*
  ANNA's *lack of modesty*)
I am so pleased about everything.

KING

  (*Trying not to be too sentimental about this*)
I am aware of your interest. I wish to say you have been of great
help to me in this endeavor. I wish to make gift.
  (*He takes a ring from his finger and holds it out to her across
  the table, not looking at her*)
I have hope you will accept.
  (*She takes it slowly and gazes at it*)
Put it on finger!
  (*Still stunned, she does not move or speak*)
Put it on! Put it on!
  (*His voice is gruff and commanding. She obeys him, slowly
  putting the ring on the index finger of her left hand.*)

ANNA

Your Majesty, I do not know what to say!

KING

When one does not know what to say, it is a time to be silent!
(*There is a pause. Both are embarrassed. The* KING *makes small talk*)
A white elephant has been discovered in the forests of Ayuthia.

ANNA

You regard that as a good omen, don't you?

KING

Yes. Everything going well with us.

ANNA
(*Warmly*)
Everything going well with us.
(*A gong sounds off left.*)

KING

Who, who, who?

KRALAHOME
(*Off-stage*)

It is I, Your Majesty.

KING

Wait, wait, wait!
(*He goes to* ANNA *with a vaguely guilty manner and amazes
her by replacing her shawl around her shoulders, then he calls
off-stage*)
Come in! Come in!

KRALAHOME
(*Entering and bowing*)

Your Majesty . . .

KING

Well, well, well?

KRALAHOME

Secret police are here. They would make report to you.

KING
(*As* ANNA *rises*)

You will wait here.
　　(*He goes out.*)

ANNA
(*Deeply concerned*)

Secret police?

KRALAHOME
(*Noticing ring*)

Your finger shines.

ANNA
(*Confused, feeling compromised*)

Yes. The King. I did not know what to say. Women in my country don't accept gifts from men. Of course, he's the King . . . Actually, it places me in a rather embarrassing position. I was intending to ask him for a rise in salary. And now . . .

KRALAHOME

And now it will be difficult to ask.

ANNA

Very. (*Turns to him*) I don't suppose you would speak to him for me—about my rise in salary, I mean.

KRALAHOME

I think I shall do this for you, because this is a strange world in which men and women can be very blind about things nearest to them.

ANNA

Thank you, Your Excellency. I don't understand what you mean, but . . .

KRALAHOME

No, but that does not matter—and I do not think he will rise your salary, anyway.

KING
(*Entering briskly*)
Ha! Good news and bad news come together. (*To* KRALAHOME) You will please to stay up all night until we have further report on item of Tuptim.

KRALAHOME

I had intended to do so, Your Majesty.
(*He bows and goes out.*)

ANNA
(*Rising*)
Perhaps I had better go, too.

KING

No! No! No! I wish to talk with you.

ANNA

Is there something wrong with Tuptim?

KING

I do not know, nor do I consider this the most important thing I must tell you. It is of greater interest that the English think highly of me. Secret police have served coffee after dinner, and listen as they talk and report conversation of British dignitaries.

ANNA
(*Shocked*)

You have been spying on your guests?

KING

How else can one find the truth? (ANNA *shakes her head disapprovingly, but he ignores this*) It appears I have made excellent impression. It is clear they do not think me barbarian.

ANNA

This is what we intended to prove.

KING

What we intended to prove! (*Suddenly switching to the second item*) Tuptim!

ANNA

What about her?

KING

She is missing from palace. You know something of this?

ANNA
(*Frightened*)

The last time I saw her, she was at the theater pavilion.

KING

That is last time anyone has seen her. She never speaks to you of running away?

ANNA
(*Evasively*)

I knew she was unhappy.

KING

Why unhappy? She is in palace of King. What is greater honor for young girl than to be in palace of King?

ANNA

Your Majesty . . . If Tuptim is caught, shall she be punished?

KING

Naturally. What would you do if you were King like me?

ANNA

I believe I would give her a chance to explain. I think I would try not to be too harsh.

KING

Hmph.

ANNA
(*Earnestly*)

Your Majesty, of what interest to you is one girl like Tuptim? She is just another woman, as a bowl of rice is just another bowl of rice, no different from any other bowl of rice.

KING

Now you understand about women! (*He picks up a book from the table*) But British poets . . .

ANNA

(*Amused*)

You have been reading poetry, Your Majesty?

KING

Out of curiosity over strange idea of love, etcetera, etcetera. I tell you this poetry is nonsense, and a silly complication of a pleasant simplicity.
   (*He sings:*)
   A woman is a female who is human,
   Designed for pleasing man, the human male.
   A human male is pleased by many women,
   And all the rest you hear is fairy tale.

ANNA

Then tell me how this fairy tale began, sir.
You cannot call it just a poet's trick.
Explain to me why many men are faithful,
And true to one wife only—

KING

They are sick!

ANNA

(*Speaking*)

But you *do* expect women to be faithful.

KING

Naturally.

ANNA

Why naturally?

KING

Because it is natural. It is like old Siamese rhyme.
 (*He sings:*)
 A girl must be like a blossom
 With honey for just one man.
 A man must live like honey bee
 And gather all he can.

 To fly from blossom to blossom
 A honey bee must be free,
 But blossom must not ever fly
 From bee to bee to bee.

ANNA

You consider this *sensible* poetry, Your Majesty?

KING

Certainly. But listen to this, from your own poet Alf-red Tenny-
sone.
 (*He reads from the book:*)
 "Now folds the lily all her sweetness up,
 And slips into the bosom of the lake . . .
 So fold thyself, my dearest, thou, and slip
 Into my bosom . . ."
 (*He looks sternly at* ANNA)
English girls are so—acrobatic?

ANNA

(*Laughing*)

Your Majesty, I don't know if I can ever make it clear to you . . .

We do not look on women as just human females. They are . . .
Well, take yourself. You are not just a human male.

KING

I am King.

ANNA

Exactly. So every man is like a King and every woman like a
Queen, when they love one another.

KING

This is a sickly idea.

ANNA

It is a beautiful idea, Your Majesty. We are brought up with it,
of course, and a young girl at her first dance . . .

KING

Young girl? They dance, too? Like I see tonight? In arms of men
not their husbands?

ANNA

Why, yes.

KING

I would not permit.

ANNA

It's very exciting when you're young, and you're sitting on a
small gilt chair, your eyes lowered, terrified that you'll be a wall
flower. Then you see two black shoes—white waistcoat—a
face . . . It speaks!
   (*She sings:*)

We've just been introduced,
I do not know you well,
But when the music started
Something drew me to your side.
So many men and girls are in each other's arms—
It made me think we might be
Similarly occupied.

> (*The* KING *sits on his throne-table watching* ANNA, *a new interest coming into his eyes*)

Shall we dance?
On a bright cloud of music shall we fly?
Shall we dance?
Shall we then say "good night" and mean "good-bye"?
Or, perchance,
When the last little star has left the sky,
Shall we still be together
With our arms around each other
And shall you be my new romance?
On the clear understanding
That this kind of thing can happen,
Shall we dance?
Shall we dance? Shall we dance?

> (ANNA, *carried away by her reminiscent mood, dances around the room until she glides by the* KING *and realizes that he is looking at her very much as he might look at one of his dancing girls. This brings her to an abrupt stop.*)

KING

Why do you stop? You dance pretty. Go on! Go on! Go on!

ANNA

Your Majesty, I—I didn't realize I was—that is, a girl would not dance while a man is looking at her.

KING

But she will dance with strange man, holding hands, etcetera, etcetera?

ANNA

Yes. Not always a strange man. Sometimes a very good friend.

KING
(*Pause*)
Good! We dance together. You show me.
(ANNA *looks a little uncertain*)
You teach! You teach! You teach!
(*He holds out his hands and she takes them.*)

ANNA

It's quite simple, the polka. You count, "one two three and one two three and one two three *and—*"

KING

One two three *and.*

ANNA
(*Singing*)
Shall we dance?

KING

One two three *and.*

ANNA

On a bright cloud of music shall we fly?

KING

One two three *and.*

ANNA

Shall we dance?

KING

One two three *and.*

ANNA

Shall we then say "good night" and mean "good-bye"?

KING

One two three, *and.*
   (*He sings:*)
Or perchance,
When the last little star has leave the sky—

ANNA

Shall we still be together,
With our arms around each other,
And shall you be my new romance?
   (KING *sings the word "romance" with her*)
On the clear understanding
That this kind of thing can happen,
Shall we dance? Shall we dance? Shall we dance?
   (*The orchestra continues, and* ANNA *resumes her lesson*)
One two three, *and*—
   (*She leads the* KING *by his hands.*)

KING

One two three—one two three—
   (*He stops*)
What is wrong? I know! I know! I forget "And." This time I
remember.

KING AND ANNA
(*Counting together as they resume dancing*)
One two three *and*, one two three *and*, one two three *and* . . .

ANNA

That's splendid, Your Majesty!

KING

Splendid. One two and—
(*He stops and protests petulantly*)
You have thrown me off count!
(*They start again*)
One two three and, one two three *and*.
(*They circle. Suddenly he stops*)
But this is not right!

ANNA

Yes, it is. You were doing . . .

KING

No! No! No! Is not right. Not the way I see Europeans dancing tonight.

ANNA

Yes, it was. It was just like that.

KING

No! . . . Were not holding two hands like this.

ANNA

(*Suddenly realizing what he means*)
Oh . . . No . . . as a matter of fact . . .

KING

Was like this. No?
> (*Looking very directly into her eyes he advances on her slowly and puts his hand on her waist.*)

ANNA
> (*Scarcely able to speak*)

Yes.

KING

Come! One two three *and*, one two three *and* . . .
> (*They dance a full refrain and dance it very well indeed, rhythmically and with spirit, both obviously enjoying it. They stop for a moment, stand off and laugh at each other. Then he wants more. He goes back to her slowly*)

Good! Come! We try again. This time I do better.

ANNA

Very well, Your Majesty.
> (*They dance again, but only for a few whirls before a gong crashes and the* KRALAHOME *bursts in.*)

KRALAHOME

Your Majesty . . .
> (*He prostrates himself.* ANNA *and the* KING *stop and separate quickly.*)

KING
> (*Furious*)

Why do you burst through my door without waiting?

KRALAHOME

We have found Tuptim.

KING

(*A pause. He folds his arms, suddenly stern.*
His speech is cold and deliberate)

Where is she?

KRALAHOME

Secret police are questioning her.

ANNA

(*Terrified for* TUPTIM)

Now you have found her, what will you do with her?

KING

(*Now miles away from her*)

I will do—what is usually done in such event.

ANNA

What is that?

KING

When it happens you will know.

(TUPTIM *dashes on, falls on her knees at* ANNA's *feet and*
clings to her skirt. Two GUARDS *run after her, two more and*
the INTERPRETER *take positions at the door.*)

TUPTIM

Mrs. Anna! Mrs. Anna! Do not let them beat me! Do not let them!
(*The* GUARDS *silence her roughly and drag her away from*
ANNA.)

KRALAHOME

She was found on Chinese sailing ship. See! She wears disguise
of priest.

KING
(*Shouting down at* TUPTIM's *prostrate, quivering figure*)
Who gave you this robe? Who? Who? Who?

KRALAHOME
It is believed she was running away with man who brought her
here from Burma.

KING
(*Deep humiliation in his voice*)
Dishonor. Dishonor. Dishonor.

KRALAHOME
He was not found on boat.

KING
(*To* TUPTIM)
Where is this man?

TUPTIM
I do not know.

KING
You will tell us where we will find him! You will tell us!

TUPTIM
I do not know.

KRALAHOME
It is believed you were lovers with this man.

TUPTIM
I was not lovers with this man.

KING

Dishonor. We will soon have truth of this man.
(*He signals the* GUARDS. *They tear the priest robe off her, leaving her back bare. One of them unwinds a stout whip.*)

TUPTIM

Mrs. Anna!

ANNA

(*Throwing herself on the man with the whip*)
Stop that! Do you hear me? Stop it!

KING

(*Coldly to* ANNA)
It would be better if you understand at once that this matter does not concern you.

ANNA

But it does. It does, dreadfully . . . because of her, and even more because of you.

KING

You waste my time.

ANNA

She's only a child. She was running away because she was unhappy. Can't you understand that? Your Majesty, I beg of you— don't throw away everything you've done. This girl hurt your vanity. She didn't hurt your heart. You haven't got a heart. You've never loved anyone. You never will.

KING

(*Pause. The* KING, *stung by* ANNA'*s words, seeks a way to hurt her in return*)

I show you! (*He snatches the whip from the guard*) Give! Give to me!

ANNA

(*Her eyes filled with horror*)

I cannot believe you are going to do this dreadful thing.

KING

You do not believe, eh? Maybe you will believe when you hear her screaming as you run down the hall! (*Pause.*)

ANNA

I am not going to run down the hall. I am going to stay here and watch you!

KING

Hold this girl! (*The two* GUARDS *grab* TUPTIM'*s arms*) I do this all myself.

ANNA

You *are* a barbarian!

KING

Down! Down! Down!

(*The* GUARDS *hold* TUPTIM *down*)

Am I King, or am I not King? Am I to be cuckold in my own palace? Am I to take orders from English schoolteacher?

ANNA

No, not orders . . .

KING

Silence! . . .
>   (*He hands the whip to the* KRALAHOME)

I am King, as I was born to be, and Siam to be governed in my way!
>   (*Tearing off his jacket*)

Not English way, not French way, not Chinese way. My way!
>   (*He flings the jacket at* ANNA *and takes back the whip from the* KRALAHOME)

Barbarian, you say. There is no barbarian worse that a weak King, and I am a strong King. You hear? Strong.
>   (*He stands over* TUPTIM, *raises the whip, meets* ANNA's *eyes, pauses, then suddenly realizing he cannot do this in front of her, he hurls the whip from him, and in deep shame, runs from the room. After a moment of silence, the* KRALAHOME *claps his hands, and the* GUARDS *yank* TUPTIM *to her feet. They are about to drag her off when the* INTERPRETER *crawls forward and speaks to the* KRALAHOME.)

INTERPRETER

The man—the lover has been found. He is dead.

TUPTIM

Dead . . . Then I shall join him soon . . . soon.
>   (*The* GUARDS *drag her off. The* INTERPRETER *follows. The* KRALAHOME *turns and looks at* ANNA *scornfully.*)

ANNA

I don't understand you—you or your King. I'll never understand him.

KRALAHOME

You! You have destroyed him. You have destroyed King . . . He cannot be anything that he was before. You have taken all this away from him. You have destroyed him. (*His voice growing louder*) You have destroyed King.

ANNA

The next boat that comes to the port of Bangkok—no matter where it goes, I shall be on it.
(*She takes the ring from her finger and holds it out to him*)
Give this back to His Majesty!
(*The* KRALAHOME *takes it. This the final humiliation for his* KING *to suffer.*)

KRALAHOME
(*Shouting, with heartbroken rage*)
I wish you have never come to Siam!

ANNA
So do I! (*She sobs*) Oh, so do I! (*She runs off.*)

INTERMEDIATE SCENE

The Palace grounds.

Townspeople and children come on, eagerly watching off stage for the approaching procession. CAPTAIN ORTON *enters and meets* PHRA ALACK.

PHRA ALACK

Captain Orton! Your ship has docked in time! We are welcoming elephant prince to Bangkok.

ORTON

White elephant, eh? So that's it. I just passed the young prince. Where is the King? I didn't see him in the procession.

PHRA ALACK

(*His face clouding*)

The King is very ill. Very ill.

> (*The procession now crosses the stage. Cymbal players, banner bearers, girls carrying huge oversized heads, and finally a dragon weaves on with four pairs of human legs propelling it. Girls dressed as strange birds dance around it. Finally* CHULALONGKORN *enters, accompanied by Amazons carrying ceremonial umbrellas. When the* PRINCE *reaches the center of the stage, the* INTERPRETER *runs on and bows before him. The* PRINCE *halts.*)

INTERPRETER

Your Highness! Go no further! Go no further!

CHULALONGKORN

What is this you say?

INTERPRETER

Your father! Your father is worse!

CHULALONGKORN

Worse?

INTERPRETER

You are to return to the palace at once.

CHULALONGKORN
(*Turning to those who are near him*)
Go on with the procession.
(*He starts off and then quickens his pace, deeply worried. The procession continues, but with all its gay spirit gone. The lights fade.*)

SCENE 5

A room in ANNA'*s house. It has been dismantled except for a few pieces of furniture. There is a crate, up center, a Victorian chair, an oriental coffee table, and another chair. As the curtain rises* LADY THIANG *is seated, looking thoughtful and worried.*

CHULALONGKORN
(*Entering*)
Mother! The Prime Minister told me you were here. I think Mrs. Anna and Louis have already left for the boat.

THIANG
No, Chulalongkorn. Some of their boxes are still here. (*She indicates the crate*) The servant said they would be back soon.
(CHULALONGKORN *walks slowly toward his mother and stands before her.*)

CHULALONGKORN
Mother, what is it with my father?

THIANG
It is his heart. (*She sits*) Also, he does not seem to want to live.

CHULALONGKORN
Mother, I am frightened. I am frightened because I love my father and also because if he dies, I shall be King, and I do not know how to be.

THIANG
Many men learn this after they become kings.

CHULALONGKORN

I have been thinking much on things Mrs. Anna used to tell us in classroom . . . Of slavery, etcetera, etcetera, and I think also on what she has said of religion, and how it is a good and noble concern that each man find for himself that which is right and that which is wrong.

THIANG

These are good things to remember, my son, and it will be good to remember the one who taught them.

LOUIS
(*Entering*)

Chulalongkorn!
(*They shake hands.* LOUIS *bows to* LADY THIANG.)

ANNA
(*Entering after* LOUIS)

Lady Thiang! How nice of you to come to say good-bye! I was down at the ship seeing that all my boxes were on. Captain Orton must sail with the tide.

THIANG

Mrs. Anna, I did not come only to say good-bye. I come for one who must see you.
(ANNA, *guessing whom she means, turns away*)
You must go to him, Mrs. Anna . . . When he heard that you were sailing, he started to write this letter.
(*She unrolls a sheet of paper she has been holding*)
All day he has been writing. It was very difficult for him, madam— very difficult. He has commanded that I bring it to you.
(ANNA *takes the letter.*)

CHULALONGKORN

Please to read it to all of us. I would like to hear what my father has said.

ANNA

(*Reading*)

"While I am lying here, I think perhaps I die. This heart, which you say I have not got, is a matter of concern. It occurs to me that there shall be nothing wrong that men shall die, for all that shall matter about man is that he shall have tried his utmost best. In looking back, I discover that you think much on those people who require that you live up to best of self. You have spoken truth to me always, and for this I have often lost my temper on you. But now I do not wish to die without saying this gratitude, etcetera, etcetera. I think it very strange that a woman shall have been most earnest help of all. But, Mrs. Anna, you must remember that you have been a very difficult woman, and much more difficult than generality."

(*Tears come into* ANNA's *voice. She looks up at* THIANG)

I must go to him!

(*She starts out*)

Come, Louis!

(*They go, followed by* THIANG *and* CHULALONGKORN.)

INTERMEDIATE SCENE

A Palace corridor.

ANNA *enters, followed by* LADY THIANG, CHULALONGKORN *and* LOUIS.

THIANG

I will see if he is awake. I will tell him you are here.
(*She goes out with* CHULALONGKORN.)

LOUIS

Mother, I thought you and the King were very angry with each other.

ANNA

We were, Louis.

LOUIS

Now he's dying—does that make you better friends?

ANNA

I suppose so, Louis. We can't hurt each other any more.

LOUIS

I didn't know he hurt you.

ANNA

When two people are as different as we are, they are almost bound to hurt each other.

LOUIS

He always frightened me.

ANNA

I wish you had known him better, Louis. You could have been great friends. (*Smiling down at him*) In some ways he was just as young as you.

LOUIS

Was he as good a king as he could have been?

ANNA

Louis, I don't think any man has ever been as good a king as he could have been . . . but this one tried. He tried very hard.
(*Pause.* LOUIS *studies her.*)

LOUIS

You really like him, don't you, Mother?

ANNA
(*Barely controlling her tears*)
Yes, Louis. I like him very much. Very much indeed. (*Looking off-stage*) We can go in now.
(*They start off as the lights fade.*)

SCENE 6

The KING'*s study.*

   The KING *lies on his bed, his head propped up slightly. His eyes are closed.* LADY THIANG *kneels beside him.* CHULALONGKORN *is crouched on the floor in front of her, and above the bed the* KRALAHOME *kneels and never takes his eyes from the* KING'*s face. Shortly after the rise of the curtain* LOUIS *enters and bows formally toward the* KING. *He is followed by* ANNA, *who curtseys and seats herself on a pile of books at the foot of the* KING'*s bed. The* KING'*s eyes open. Presently he addresses* ANNA.

KING

Many months . . . Many months I do not see you, Mrs. Anna. And now I die.

ANNA

Oh, no, Your Majesty.

KING

This is not scientific, Mrs. Anna. I know if I die or do not die. You are leaving Siam?
   (ANNA *nods*)
When?

ANNA

Very soon, Your Majesty. In fact, I can stay only a few minutes more.

KING

You are glad for this?
   (ANNA *can find no answer*)
People of Siam—royal children, etcetera, are not glad, and all are in great affliction of your departure.

ANNA

I shall miss them.

KING

You shall miss them, but you shall be leaving. I too am leaving.
But I am not walking onto a boat with my own feet, of my own
free will. I am just . . . leaving.
(*His eyes close, but he has seen where* ANNA *is sitting*)
Why is your head above mine?
(ANNA *rises, and* LOUIS *removes one of the books from the pile.*
As ANNA *sits again,* LOUIS *kneels beside her*)
I am not afraid of that which is happening to me.
(*He whistles the melody of the "Whistling Song."* ANNA *looks*
at him with quick surprise. He smiles and explains:)
You teach Chulalongkorn. Chulalongkorn teach me . . . "Make
believe you brave"—is good idea, always.

ANNA

You are very brave, Your Majesty. Very brave.

KING

(*Taking from his finger the ring he has given her once before*)
Here is—something belonging to you. Put it on.
(*He holds it out to her*)
Put it on! Put it on! Put it on!
(*Then, for the first time in his life, he puts a plea in his voice*)
Please . . . wear it.
(ANNA *takes it, unable to speak, and puts it on. After a moment,*
the children enter, accompanied by the Amazons. LADY THIANG
rises hastily to quiet the children. The KING *hears them*)
My children? Tell them to come here.
(*They hurry in and prostrate themselves before their father*)
Good evening, my children.

CHILDREN
(*Together*)

Good evening, my father.
(*Then they rush to* ANNA, *cluttering around her, hugging her,
greeting her in overlapping speeches*)
Oh, Mrs. Anna. Do not go! We are happy to see you. We have
missed you so much, Mrs. Anna. Will you stay, Mrs. Anna? Do
not go away!

LADY THIANG

Stop! Stop this noise! Did you come to see your father or Mrs.
Anna?

KING
(*He has watched the children with interest*)

It is all right, Lady Thiang. It is suitable.
(*The children settle on the floor around* ANNA)
Was it not said to me that someone has written a farewell letter
to Mrs. Anna?

THIANG

Princess Ying Yaowalak has composed letter to Mrs. Anna. She
cannot write. She only make up words.
(PRINCESS YING YAOWALAK *stands up.*)

KING

Speak letter now. (*The* PRINCESS *is uncertain*) Say it! Say it! Say it!

YING YAOWALAK
(*Reciting her "letter"*)

Dear friend and teacher: My goodness gracious, do not go away!
We are in great need of you. We are like one blind. Do not let us
fall down in darkness. Continue good and sincere concern for

us, and lead us in right road. Your loving pupil, Princess Ying
Yaowalak.

(ANNA *rises, unable to speak, rushes to the little girl and hugs her.*)

CHILDREN

Please to stay, Mrs. Anna. Do not leave us! We cannot live without you! We are afraid, Mrs. Anna. We are afraid without you.

KING

Hush, children. When you are afraid, make believe you brave.
(*To* ANNA) You tell them how you do. You tell them. Let it be
last thing you teach.

CHILDREN

(*As* ANNA *looks uncertainly at the* KING)
Tell us then, Mrs. Anna. What to do when afraid? You teach us.

ANNA

(*With a great effort to control her tears, she sings:*)
Whenever I feel afraid
I hold my head erect.
  (*The children hold their heads up in imitation of her*)
And whistle a happy tune
So no one will suspect
I'm afraid.
While shivering in my shoes
I strike a careless pose
  (*Her eyes go to* LOUIS, *who strikes the "careless pose." All the
  children imitate him*)
And whistle a happy tune
And no one ever knows
I'm afraid.

KING
(*Speaking over the music*)
You see? You make believe you brave, and you whistle. Whistle!
(*The children look at him, not comprehending. He addresses* ANNA)
You show them!
(ANNA *whistles. The* KING *motions to the children. They all try
to whistle, but cannot. Finally, something like a whistle comes
from the twins. This is too much for* ANNA. *She kneels and
throws her arms around them, weeping freely. The sound of a
boat whistle is heard off in the distance.*)

LOUIS
(*Crossing to* ANNA *and tapping her shoulder*)
Mother . . . It's the boat! It's time!
(*The children look at her anxiously. She rises.*)

CHILDREN
Do not go, Mrs. Anna. Please do not go.
(*Pause. Then, suddenly,* ANNA *starts to remove her bonnet.*)

ANNA
Louis, please go down and ask Captain Orton to take all our boxes
off the ship. And have everything moved back into our house.
(LOUIS *runs off eagerly. The children break into shouts of joy.*)

KING
Silence!
(*At the note of anger in his voice, the children, wives,* LADY
THIANG—*all fall prostrate*)
Is no reason for doing of this demonstration for schoolteacher
realizing her duty, for which I pay her exorbitant monthly salary
of twenty . . . five pounds! Further, this is disorganized behavior
for bedroom of dying King!

(*To* CHULALONGKORN, *who has remained crouching below the bed*)

Chulalongkorn! Rise!

(*The boy rises*)

Mrs. Anna, you take notes.

(*He hands her a notebook, and she sits on the pile of books*)

You take notes from—next King.

(LADY THIANG *lifts her head as the* KING *continues to the momentarily tongue-tied* PRINCE)

Well, well, well? Suppose you are King! Is there nothing you would do?

CHULALONGKORN
(*In a small, frightened voice*)

I . . . would make proclamations.

KING

Yes, yes.

CHULALONGKORN

First, I would proclaim for coming New Year—fireworks.

(*The* KING *nods his approval*)

Also boat races.

KING

Boat races? Why would you have boat races with New Year celebration?

CHULALONGKORN

I like boat races.

(*His confidence is growing. He speaks a little faster*)

And, Father, I would make a second proclamation.

(*He swallows hard in preparation for this one.*)

KING

Well, go on! What is second proclamation? Make it! Make it!

CHULALONGKORN

Regarding custom of bowing to King in fashion of lowly toad.
   (*He starts to pace, very like his father*)
I do not believe this is good thing, causing embarrassing fatigue of
body, degrading experience for soul, etcetera, etcetera, etcetera. . . .
This is bad thing.
   (*He crosses his arms defiantly*)
I believe.
   (*He is losing his nerve a little*)
You are angry with me, my father?

KING

Why do you ask question? If you are King you are King. You do
not ask questions of sick man—
   (*Glaring at* ANNA)
Nor of woman!
   (*Pointing an accusing finger at her*)
This proclamation against bowing I believe to be your fault!

ANNA

Oh, I hope so, Your Majesty. I do hope so.
   (*Music of "Something Wonderful" starts to be played here—
   very softly.*)

CHULALONGKORN
   (*Clapping his hands twice*)
Up! Rise up!
   (*A few rise. The others raise their heads, but are uncertain
   whether they should obey him.*)

KING

Up! Up! Up!
(*They all rise quickly, wives, Amazons, children*)
Two lines, like soldiers.
(*They line up*)
It has been said there shall be no bowing for showing respect of
King. It has been said by one who has . . . been trained for royal
government.
(*His head sinks back on the pillow, and his voice on the last
word was obviously weak.*)

CHULALONGKORN
(*His voice stronger and more decisive*)
No bowing like toad. No crouching. No crawling. This does not
mean, however, that you do not show respect for King.
(*The KING's eyes close*)
You will stand with shoulders square back, and chin high . . .
like this.
(ANNA *turns and notices that the* KING's *eyes are closed. The*
KRALAHOME, *knowing that he has died, crawls on his knees to
the head of the bed, and crouches there, heartbroken, and not
wishing other people to see that he is weeping.* CHULALONGKORN
continues his instructions)
You will bow to me—the gentlemen, in this way, only bending
the waist.
(*As he shows them and continues speaking,* ANNA *glides to the
head of the bed, and feels the* KING's *hand. Then she comes
around the foot of the bed and sinks to the floor beside him,
taking his hand and kissing it*)
The ladies will make dip, as in Europe.
(*He starts to show them a curtsey, but cannot*)
Mother—

(LADY THIANG *crosses to the center and drops a low curtsey before the women. As the music swells, all the women and girls carefully imitate her, sinking to the floor as the curtain falls, a final obeisance to the dead* KING, *a gesture of allegiance to the new one.*)

Curtain

PHOTOGRAPH CREDITS

"An impressive show.... one of the most beautiful in memory and also tasteful, colorful, sentimental, melodic and generally entertaining."

– Variety

To learn more about *The King and I*
and the other great musicals available for production
through R&H Theatricals, please visit:

www.rnh.com

or contact

229 W. 28th St.,
11th Floor
New York, NY 10001

THEATRICALS

Phone: (212) 564-4000
Fax: (212) 268-1245
Email: theatre@rnh.com

The R&H logo is a trademark of Imagem, C.V.